STEP-BY-STEP
CRAFTS
FOR
CHILDREN

- MAKING JEWELRY
- MAKING KITES
- MAKING CARDS
- MAKING BOOKS

KINGfISHER

NEW YORK

KINGFISHER
Larousse Kingfisher Chambers Inc.
95 Madison Avenue
New York, New York 10016

First published in 2000
The material in this edition was previously published in four individual volumes
as *Step-by-Step Making Jewelry* (Sara Grisewood), *Making Kites* (David Michael),
Making Cards (Charlotte Stowell), *Making Books* (Charlotte Stowell)

2 4 6 8 10 9 7 5 3 1
1TR/1199/SC/(HBM)/128JMA

LIBRARY OF CONGRESS CATALOGING-IN-PUBLICATION DATA
has been applied for.

ISBN 0-7534-5300-2

Editor: Deri Robins
Designer: Ben White
Illustrator: Jim Robins
Photographers: Rolf Cornell (SCL Photographic Services),
Steve Shott, Steven Sullivan
Cover designer: Terry Woodley

Printed in Hong Kong

MAKING JEWELRY
5 – 44

CONTENTS

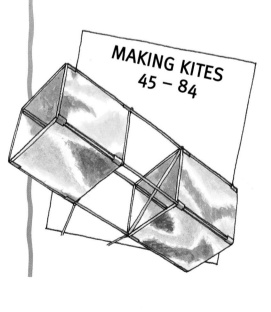

MAKING KITES
45 – 84

MAKING CARDS
85 – 124

MAKING BOOKS
125 – 164

STEP-BY-STEP

MAKING JEWELRY

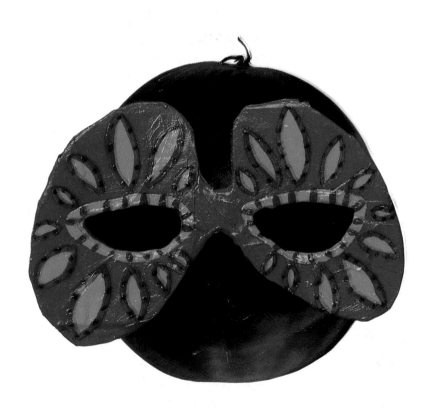

MAKING JEWELRY

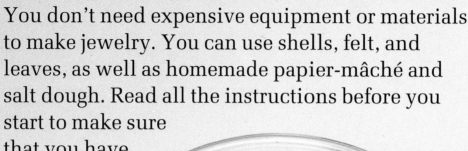

You don't need expensive equipment or materials to make jewelry. You can use shells, felt, and leaves, as well as homemade papier-mâché and salt dough. Read all the instructions before you start to make sure that you have everything you need.

Paint

Varnish

Flour

Wallpaper paste

Rolling pin

Colored clay

Salt

Special Things

Findings are the special fastenings used to make jewelry. Necklaces can be tied with a knot, but you'll need findings for pins and earrings.

Craft stores sell findings, as well as beads, sequins, and fake gemstones.

Paper clips are ideal for pendant hooks—just stick them into the jewelry before baking. For threading heavy beads, buy a strong thread, such as linen carpet thread.

Tools of the Trade

You'll need scissors, a craft knife, glue (a safe but strong epoxy glue), a pencil, metal ruler, masking tape, sewing thread, and needles.

An ordinary knife, fork and spoon, and a rolling pin make ideal tools for modeling. Work on an old board. Bake beads on metal skewers.

Buy colored clay, such as Fimo. Keep paper and wallpaper paste on hand for papier-mâché, and flour, salt, and water for salt dough (see page 10). You'll also need paints, brushes, and varnish (see pages 12–13).

String

Needle

Felt

Strong thread

Shells

Skewer

Brush

Newspaper

Craft knife

Modeling tools

Findings

Scissors

Epoxy glue

Bought beads

Leaves

9

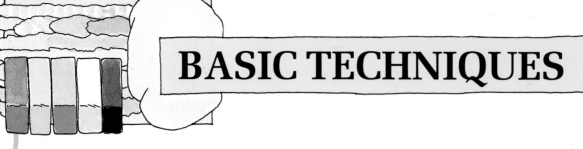

BASIC TECHNIQUES

Colored clay is ideal for making jewelry and doesn't even need a coat of paint. Other modeling materials, such as salt dough and papier-mâché, can be made at home very cheaply.

Making Salt Dough

Stir together ½ cup of salt with 3 cups of sifted flour. Slowly add between 7½ and 12 fl. ounces of warm water.

Mix together to make a soft dough. Knead until smooth, then leave it in a plastic bag for half an hour before using.

Bake your pieces at 340°F. Beads and pins take between ½–1½ hours. Ask an adult to tap them—if they sound hollow, they are ready.

Most wallpaper pastes contain fungicide, which is poisonous. Always buy a nonfungicidal paste and follow the instructions on the package carefully.

Making Papier-Mâché

Old cereal boxes will make ideal cardboard bases for your jewelry. Cover your base with layers of torn newspaper dipped in wallpaper paste. The smaller the strips, the smoother your jewelry will be. Let the papier-mâché dry between layers.

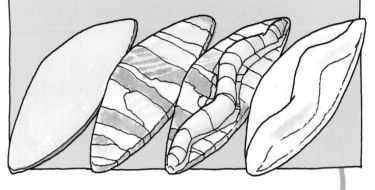

Using Colored Clay

You can buy colored clay from craft and toy stores—it even comes in metallic and fluorescent colors! Always follow the instructions on the package before baking. Work on a board and clean your work surface before you change colors.

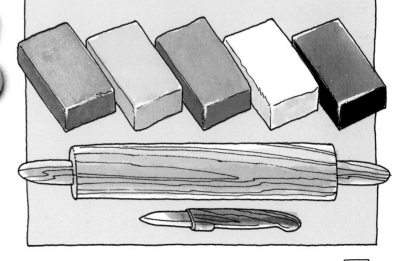

FINISHING TOUCHES

Finish off salt-dough and papier-mâché pieces by painting and varnishing them. Varnish also stops decorations from falling off and protects fragile objects, such as leaves—after all, painting isn't the only way to decorate your jewelry.

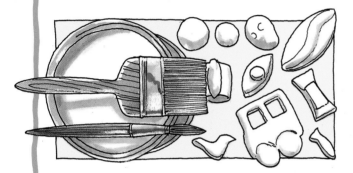

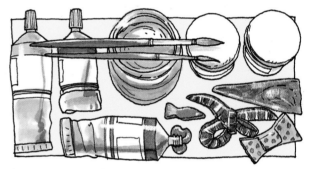

Paints and Brushes

Always let salt-dough jewelry cool and papier-mâché objects dry before painting. Apply a coat of white latex paint first so that you have a smooth, white surface to decorate. It will keep newsprint from showing through on your papier-mâché pieces.

Acrylic paints are best if you want really dazzling results, but poster paints give bright colors, too, and are much cheaper. Latex, acrylics, and poster paints are all water-based, so all you'll need to clean your brushes is plenty of water.

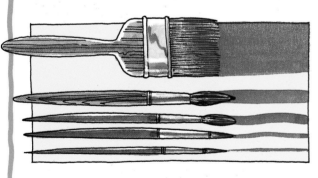

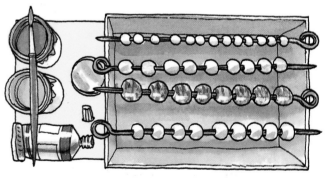

Keep a selection of brushes handy. A large, thick brush is best for the base coat, but you'll need finer ones for painting details, especially on homemade beads.

When you have lots of beads to paint, thread them on metal skewers. Rest the needle across an open shoe box, then paint. Leave the beads on the needle until they are all dry.

Using a cloth to rub gold paint on top of green will make your jewelry look like a valuable antique!

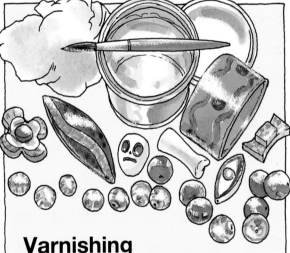

Tricks with Paint

After the latex paint, apply a base color. When this is dry, use a fine brush to paint a pattern on top.

Try smearing paint onto wood with your fingers. This gives an uneven and unusual stained effect.

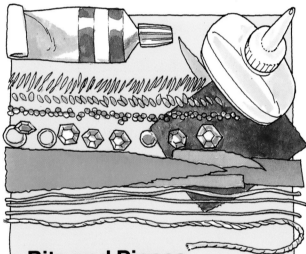

Bits and Pieces

You can glue all sorts of daring decorations onto your jewelry. Use a strong epoxy glue or ordinary white glue.

Gems, natural objects (such as seeds), and even string can all be used as unusual surface decorations. The only limit is your imagination!

Varnishing

Give all your painted jewelry a glossy coat of polyurethane varnish. It makes the paint really shine and stops it from chipping.

When varnishing, make sure there is enough air in the room. Varnish can be dangerous if you breathe in too much of it. Always keep the window wide open.

BRILLIANT PINS

These pins will really brighten up a jacket or coat! We used colored clay for the balloon and the musical pins and added layers of clay to make raised patterns—this is called "relief" decoration.

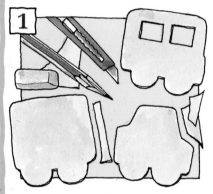
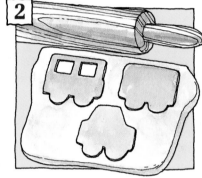
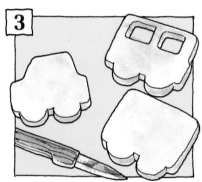

Salt-dough Pins

Draw and cut out simple shapes on cardboard to use as templates for your pins.

Roll out a slab of salt dough to about $\frac{1}{3}$ inch thick. Put the templates on the dough.

Now cut around the templates. You can cut out holes for windows too, if you want.

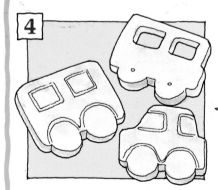

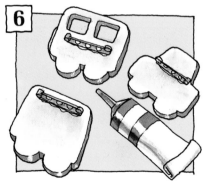

To mark the edges of the windows or wheels, dig into the dough with a fingernail or knife.

Bake the pins in the oven. Leave them to cool, then paint and varnish the fronts.

Stick a finding to the back, using a strong glue. Let the glue dry, then wear your pin!

14

To make this hot-air balloon, you'll need to roll very thin layers of colored clay. Try not to smudge them!

Salt dough is just the thing for these chunky, colorful pins.

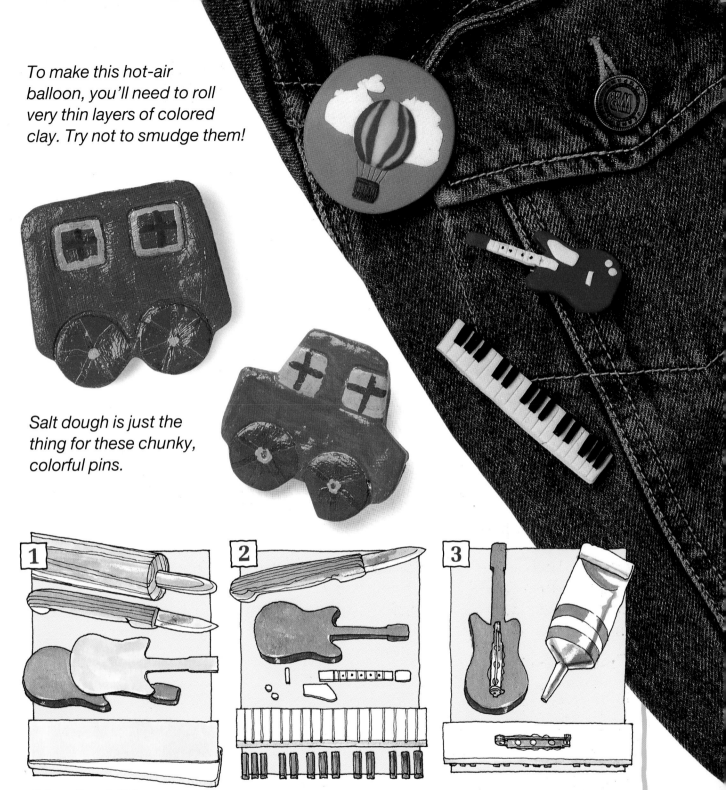

Musical Pins

1 Make templates for the guitar and keyboard. Place them on $\frac{1}{4}$-inch-thick colored clay and cut around them.

2 Cut out piano keys and the guitar trimmings and press into place. Mark piano keys and guitar frets with a knife.

3 Bake the pins in the oven. When they are cool, use a strong glue to attach findings to the back.

15

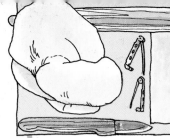

FLOWERS AND BOWS

Salt-dough flowers and bows make pretty pins. Bake all your pieces together, leave to cool, and then paint and varnish. Finally, glue findings to the backs. Brooches make wonderful presents—if you can bear to give these away!

Bows

Roll out some salt dough to $\frac{1}{4}$ inch thick. Then use a knife to cut a strip ($\frac{1}{2}$ in. x 6 in.), like a salt-dough ribbon.

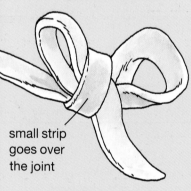

small strip goes over the joint

Loop the strip into a bow, as if it were a ribbon. Join together wherever one layer overlaps another—just dab with water and press gently. Use an extra scrap to cover the center.

To make a bow-tie pin, cut out a basic bow-tie shape and a small rectangle (for the "knot") from salt dough. Stick the knot on with a dab of water.

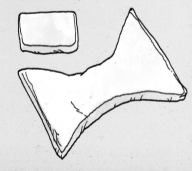

Flowers

Make a cardboard template for the petals. Cut out about ten petals from salt dough.

Overlap the petals to make a circle. Dab with water and smooth the joints.

Press a blob of dough in the center of each flower to hide where the petals joined.

For another kind of flower, cut the base with a cookie cutter. Stick four diamond-shaped petals on top.

You can also make flowers by sticking four smaller petals on top of four larger ones.

RINGS AND THINGS

Papier-mâché is perfect for making fun, chunky jewelry. You can decorate rings with jewels made from scrunched-up tissue paper. Finally, use bright paints in different colors. Let each coat of paint dry before using a new color. Always make sure your bangles and rings are big enough to slide on and off your wrist and fingers easily.

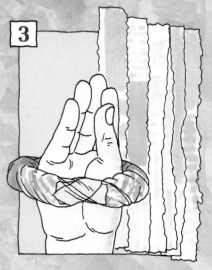

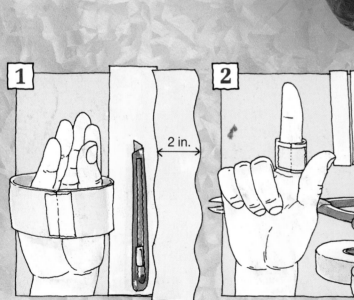

1
Cut two strips of thin cardboard. Give one a wavy edge. Ask a friend to hold each strip around your hand and tape it together for you.

2 in.

2
Cut narrower strips to make rings. Wrap them around your finger, so they slide off easily, then tape the ends together as before.

3
For a chunky bracelet, take six strips of newspaper and twist them together. Wrap this rope around your wrist and tape as before.

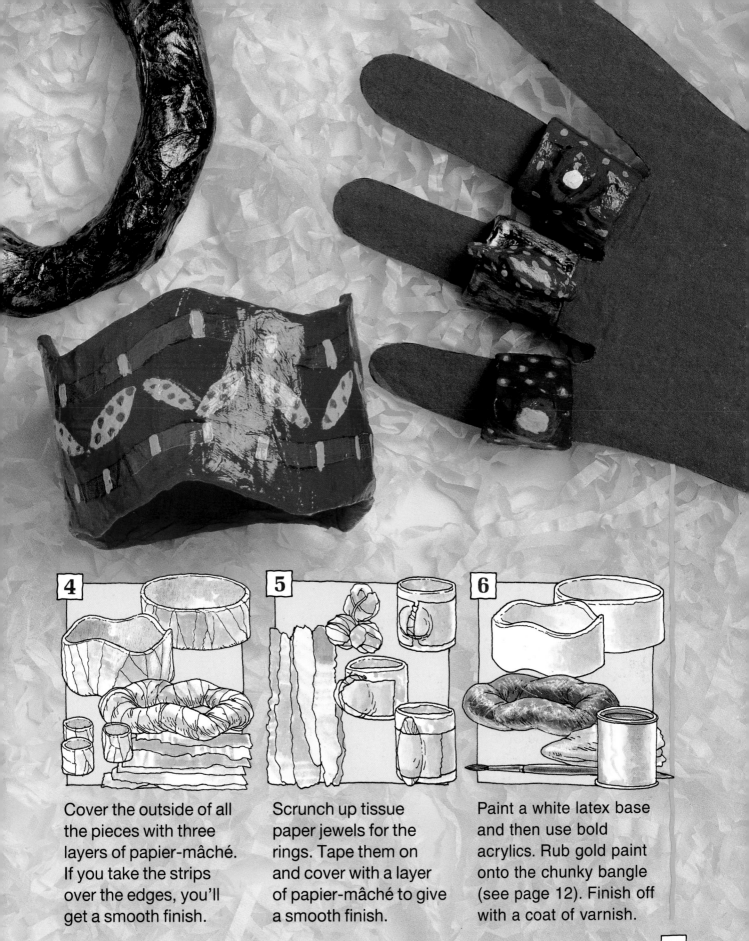

4 Cover the outside of all the pieces with three layers of papier-mâché. If you take the strips over the edges, you'll get a smooth finish.

5 Scrunch up tissue paper jewels for the rings. Tape them on and cover with a layer of papier-mâché to give a smooth finish.

6 Paint a white latex base and then use bold acrylics. Rub gold paint onto the chunky bangle (see page 12). Finish off with a coat of varnish.

19

BEAD NECKLACES

Salt-dough beads look great threaded together with beads bought from craft stores.
Try making round beads, then go for new shapes, such as the Egyptian eyes. Mix different types together—string big, homemade beads with tiny colored glass ones.

1
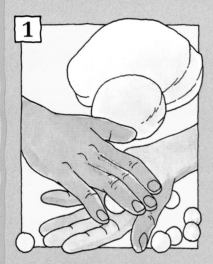
Pinch off a small piece of salt dough and roll it into a ball in your palm.

2
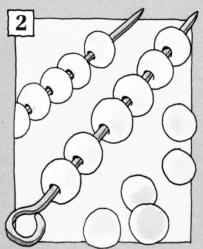
Push each bead onto a metal skewer. Smooth each bead's surface.

3
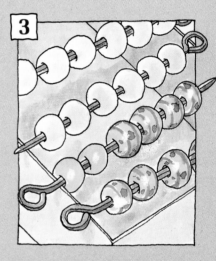
Bake the beads on their skewers. Paint and varnish when cool.

Threading Beads

Take a length of strong thread. Tape down one end with masking tape (so your beads don't fall off), then thread on the beads with a needle. Peel off the tape and knot the ends of thread together. Feed the leftover thread neatly back through the beads.

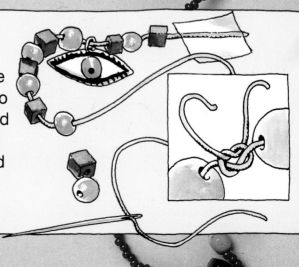

Beads don't have to be round— these are shaped like Egyptian eyes! Push in a metal paper clip before baking and thread them by the hooks.

For a lucky charm, tie red ribbon to a spare Egyptian eye bead. Pin the ribbon on with a safety pin.

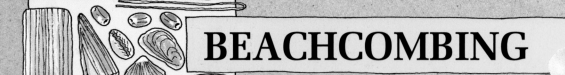

BEACHCOMBING

The beach is a treasure trove for jewelers! But shells can be tricky to drill, so it is usually easier to buy them with ready-drilled holes from a craft store. Show off the shells by trying out these different ways of threading.

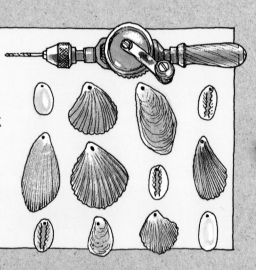

Drilling

If you do want to use shells that you've collected yourself, ask an adult to drill holes in them for you. They will need to use a drill with a fine bit. Always wash the shells first.

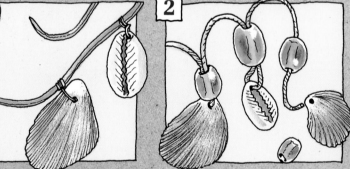

1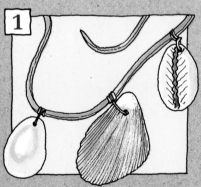

2

3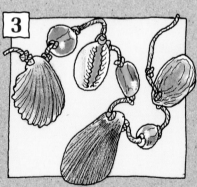

Threading Shells

With some thread, tie about three shells to the middle of a leather thong. Try using a colored thong.

Thread a bead, then a shell, then go back through the bead. Leave a space before threading the next two.

Knot some string, thread on a shell, then knot again. Leave a space, then repeat with a bead.

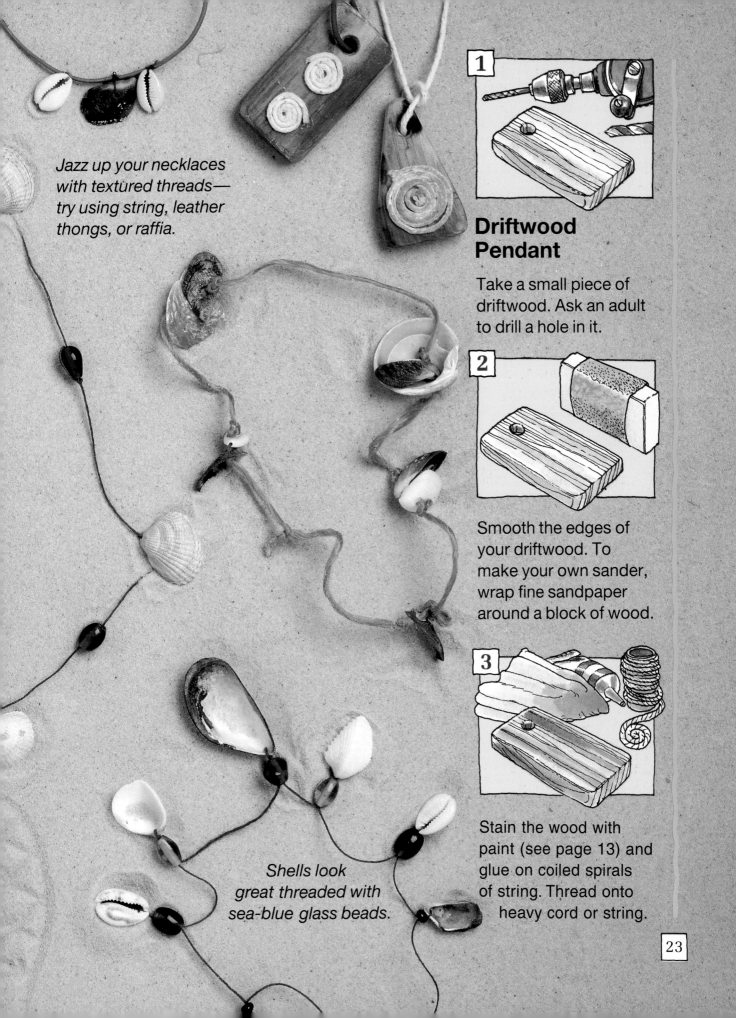

Jazz up your necklaces with textured threads— try using string, leather thongs, or raffia.

Driftwood Pendant

1

Take a small piece of driftwood. Ask an adult to drill a hole in it.

2

Smooth the edges of your driftwood. To make your own sander, wrap fine sandpaper around a block of wood.

3

Stain the wood with paint (see page 13) and glue on coiled spirals of string. Thread onto heavy cord or string.

Shells look great threaded with sea-blue glass beads.

EARRINGS

You can wear earrings whether your ears are pierced or not. Craft stores sell clip-on earring findings as well as ones for pierced ears. Glue clip-ons to the back of the finished earring.

Pierced Ears

Findings for pierced ears have two parts. The hook is the part that goes through your ear. It slips onto the pin. There are two different kinds of pin—head pins and eye pins.

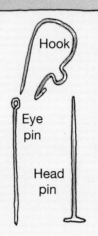

Hook

Eye pin

Head pin

Head pins are used for bead earrings. The head stops the beads from falling off (see page 29). When the beads are in place, bend around the top of the pin with tweezers to make an eye for the hook.

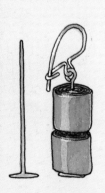

Eye pins are used for papier-mâché or salt-dough earrings. They have an eye, but no head. Stick them into the earring so the eye pokes out at the top.

Salt Dough

Shape the salt dough—tiny fish and birds are easy and fun to do. Before baking, push in an eye pin. After baking, painting, and varnishing your earrings, slip the eye pin over a hook.

Papier-Mâché

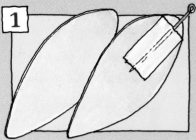

1 Start with two shaped cardboard bases. Tape an eye pin to each base, so that the eye pokes out of the top.

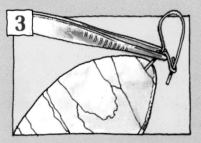

2 Cover with two layers of papier-mâché. Make relief decorations with scrunched-up paper. When dry, cover with latex, paint, and varnish.

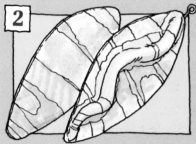

3 Slide the earring pin onto the hook by its eye. Squeeze the hook's wire so the pin won't slip off.

For a really snazzy special effect, rub on sparkling gold paint before varnishing.

PIRATE ATTACK!

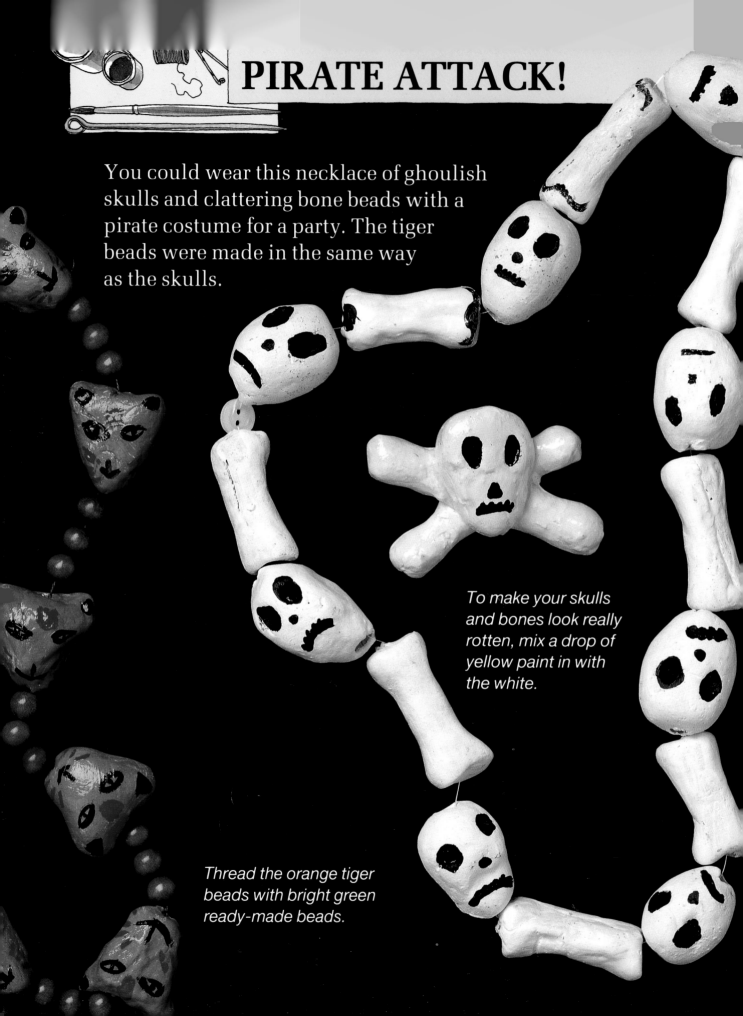

You could wear this necklace of ghoulish skulls and clattering bone beads with a pirate costume for a party. The tiger beads were made in the same way as the skulls.

To make your skulls and bones look really rotten, mix a drop of yellow paint in with the white.

Thread the orange tiger beads with bright green ready-made beads.

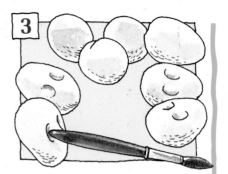 **1**

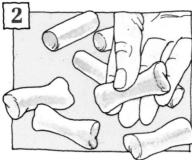 **2**

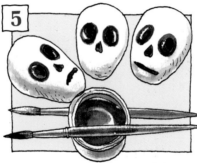 **3**

With your hands, roll some salt dough into a sausage shape about 12 inches long. Cut into eight pieces.

Shape each piece to look like a bone. It's best to pinch the dough in at the middle of the bone and at both ends.

Roll eight balls of salt dough for the skulls. Squeeze in the cheeks. Use the end of a brush to make eye sockets.

 **4**

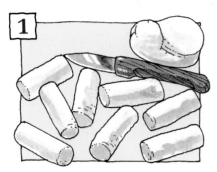 **5**

 **6**

Push all the beads onto metal skewers and bake in the oven. When cool, give everything a coat of white paint.

For extra ghoul-appeal, use black paint to make the skulls' eyes, noses, and mouths really stand out! Then varnish.

Thread the skulls and bones. Tie the ends of the thread to a button —it keeps the beads on as you work.

Bony Brooch

Join two bones in the middle with a dab of water, as shown. Press a skull on top.

Smooth the back of the brooch surface. Bake, paint, and varnish, then glue on a finding.

SWEET TOOTH

Use colored clay to make this delicious "candy" jewelry. Don't leave your beads lying around though—they look so realistic that someone might end up eating them!

1 Break off small lumps of clay. Roll into balls, then knock each one on your work surface to flatten the edges until you get a cube shape.

2 Make striped "candies" by rolling out layers of different-colored clays. Press them on top of each other, then cut into squares.

3 Roll some clay into a long sausage with your fingers. Wrap a new color around it and press gently. Smooth out where they join.

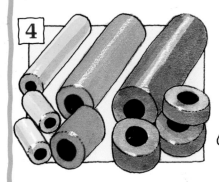

4 Cut the sausage shape into candy-sized beads. Make more in the same way, but change the thickness and cut to different lengths.

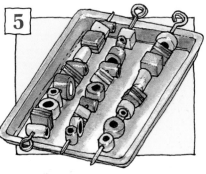

5 Push all your beads onto metal skewers and bake them in the oven, on a baking tray. Follow the instructions on the package carefully.

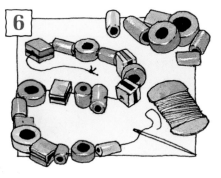

6 When the beads are all cool, thread them onto fine elastic, then knot the ends. You can make a necklace and a matching bracelet.

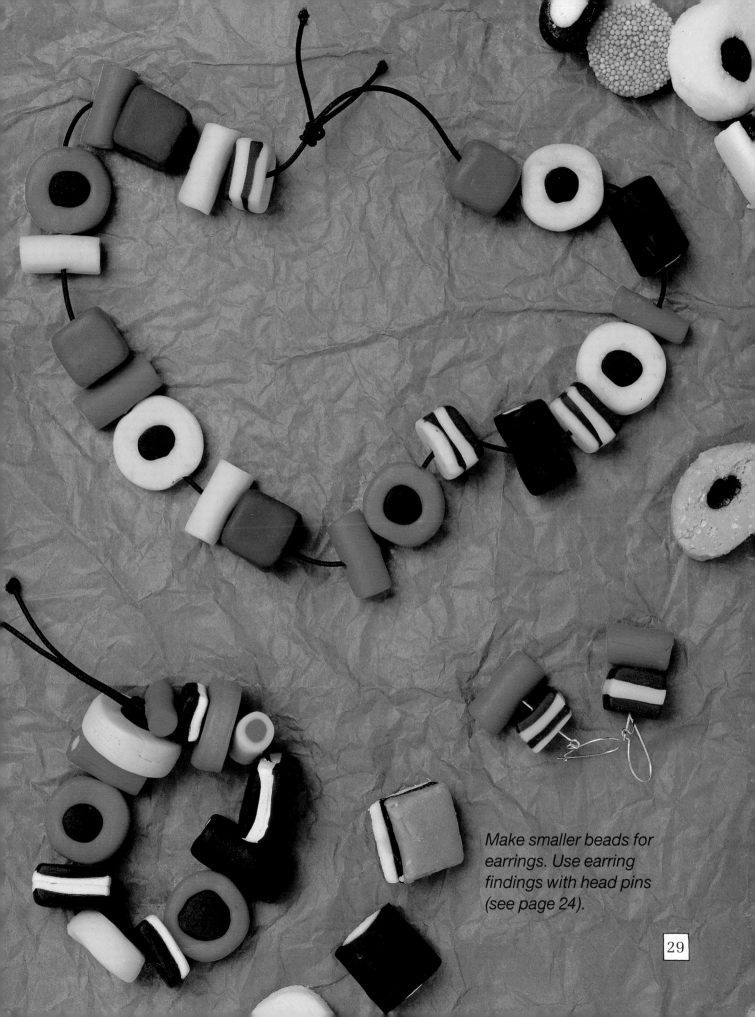

Make smaller beads for earrings. Use earring findings with head pins (see page 24).

29

PAPER JEWELRY

Rolled paper beads may look delicate, but the wallpaper paste makes them surprisingly strong. Try using all sorts of colored paper in lots of different thicknesses, as well as newspapers and old magazines.

1

Make several cardboard templates. Rectangles make simple tube beads. To make oval beads, use a triangle. For fat beads use long templates. For long beads use wide templates.

2

Use the templates to cut out paper triangles and rectangles. To save time, fold the paper in an accordion and draw around the template. Then cut out lots of paper strips at once.

For earring beads with a large hole, use an eye pin (see page 24), and bend back the pin with tweezers.

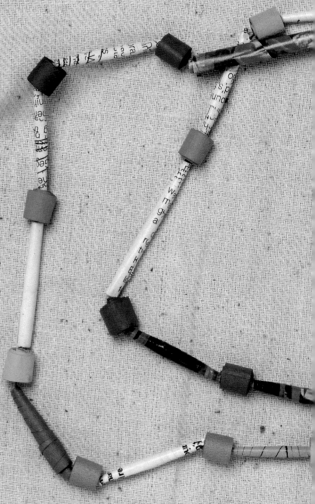

3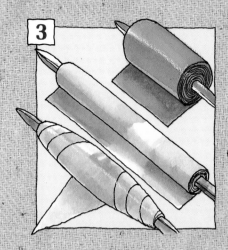

4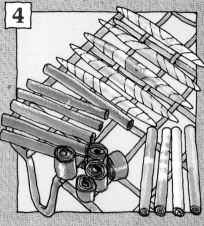

5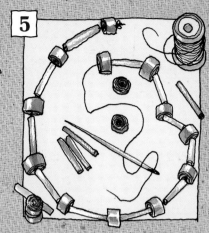

Coat both sides of each strip with paste, then roll around a skewer. Roll triangles from their base and rectangles from their short edge.

Slide the beads off the skewer and place on a wire rack to give the paste time to dry. There's no need to varnish the beads.

Thread the beads through their skewer holes, using strong cotton thread. Finish off by tying the thread with a double knot.

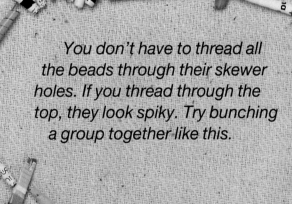

You don't have to thread all the beads through their skewer holes. If you thread through the top, they look spiky. Try bunching a group together like this.

BACK TO NATURE

Natural objects make delicate, unusual necklaces. Collect seeds and leaves outdoors, or raid the kitchen for bay leaves and melon seeds—anything you can find! You'll need to wash melon seeds, place them on paper towels, and leave them to dry in a warm place for a few days. A coat of varnish will give the bay leaves extra strength and shine.

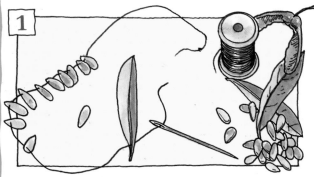

1 Thread a needle. Knot the end of the thread and then push the needle through about ten melon seeds. Then thread a bay leaf.

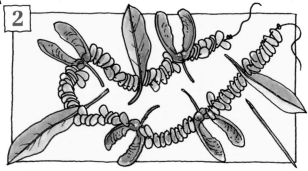

2 Alternate rows of melon seeds and tree seeds or bay leaves. Tie a knot at the end to secure all the seeds and leaves.

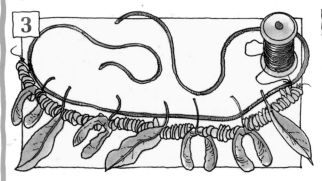

3 Take a length of cord about $2\frac{1}{2}$ feet long. Position the string of seeds in the middle. Now cut another piece of thread and use it to tie one end of the row of seeds to the cord.

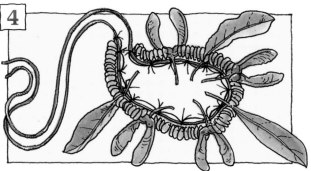

4 Use a double knot to attach the seeds to the cord, about every $\frac{3}{4}$ inch along, until you reach the end. Knot the ends of the cord and your necklace is ready to wear!

Always ask an adult before you gather seeds. Some of them are poisonous.

FELT FRUITS

Squares of felt come in just about every color of the rainbow. Felt is fabulous for making mouthwatering fruits like these.

Felt fruits look great pinned to clothes, bags, or floppy sunhats. Or why not display them in a mini fruit basket?

1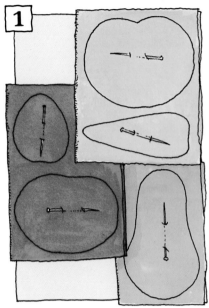

Draw templates for the tangerine, pear, carrot, tomato, and strawberry on paper. Cut them out and pin to scraps of felt.

2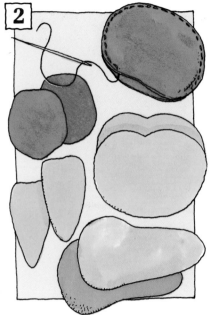

Cut around each template twice. Sew the two halves of each fruit together, leaving a small opening.

3

Stuff each fruit with cotton balls, then sew up the gap. Cut out felt leaves and sew to the top of each fruit.

4

To finish, sew tiny colored beads to the strawberries. Push a tiny safety pin through the back of each fruit.

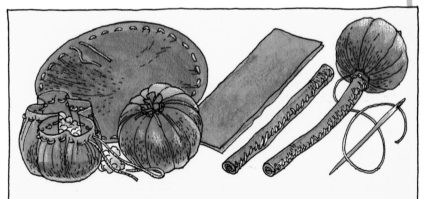

A Bunch of Cherries

Stitch around a small circle of red felt, then tighten the thread to pull the felt into a ball. Stuff the opening with cotton balls, then finish sewing up the cherry.

Cut thin strips of felt for the stems. Fold in half and stitch down the edge. Sew one to each cherry and pin together in bunches. Add stems to the strawberries, too.

GROOVY GLASSES

Make these swanky glasses for when you feel like some
larger-than-life dressing up! Design them in the
wackiest shapes you can imagine. Use bold,
vivid colors and paint on wild patterns.
For the sunburst glasses, build papier-
mâché sunrays across the eye holes.
Make sure you leave the slits wide
enough for you to see through.

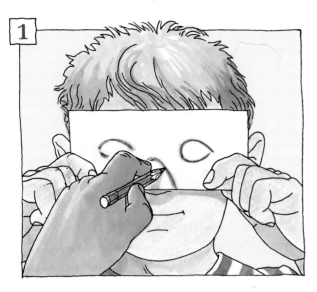

1

Measure across your face and cut a piece of thin cardboard to this width. Hold it to your face and ask a friend to mark where your eyes and nose are.

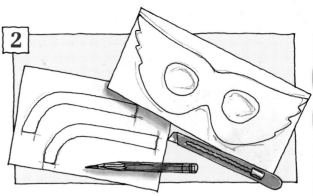

2

Draw the outline of your glasses and cut them out carefully with a craft knife. Then measure and cut out a pair of arms for your glasses.

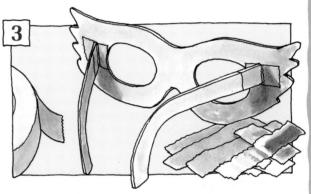

3

Make a hinge by taping the arms to the glasses with masking tape. Cover with about three layers of papier-mâché. Keep the arm hinges moving as the layers dry so you will be able to fold your finished glasses.

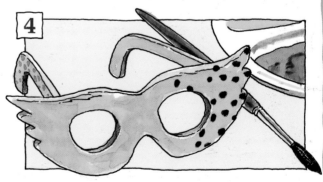

4

Coat the glasses with white latex, then paint a dazzling pattern in bright acrylic paints. Finish off your groovy glasses with a glossy layer of varnish.

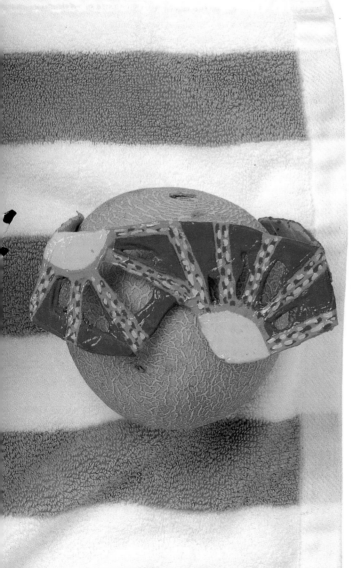

MEGA MEDALS

Ever felt you deserved a medal? Well, now you can wear one that's big enough for everyone to see! The giant pocket watch is papier-mâché, too.

Hang the medals on lengths of ribbon and use gold string for the watch chain.

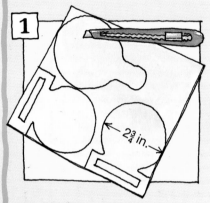

1 Draw the shapes onto thin cardboard and cut them out with a craft knife.

2¾ in.

2 Cover the cardboard bases with two layers of papier-mâché. For a raised watch face, tape on a smaller circle and cover with one more layer.

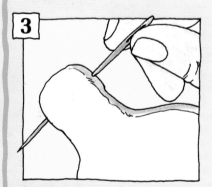

3 Paint and varnish your pieces. Use a darning needle to pierce a hole through the top of the watch for the chain. Reopen the hole after each coat of paint or varnish.

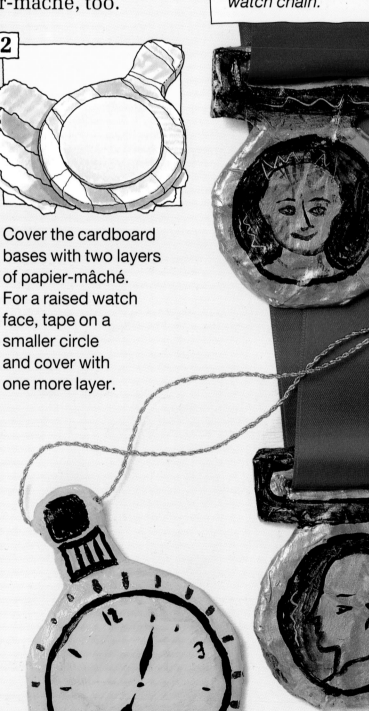

AZTEC JEWELRY

The Aztec people lived in South America hundreds of years ago and their goldsmiths were famous for their dazzling jewelry. Make your own glittering Aztec necklace and a matching ceremonial headdress, encrusted with gems. Finish off with a flourish of bright, colored feathers.

1

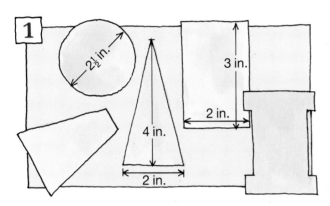

Cut out the cardboard necklace parts —you'll need a circle, two rectangles, and two triangles. Snip the tops of both triangles. Cut into the sides of one of the rectangles, as shown.

2

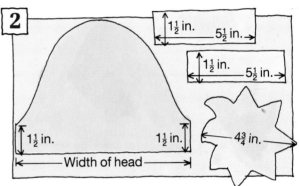

Measure the width of your head, then draw and cut out the headdress front, sides, and star. Bend the headdress so it fits the shape of your head, and then tape on the sides.

3

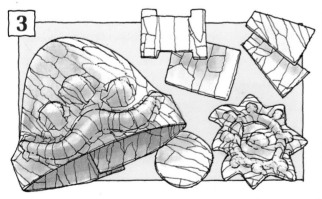

Cover all the shapes with three layers of papier-mâché. Tape scrunched-up paper to the headdress and star for raised decoration (see page 25). Cover with a layer of papier-mâché.

4

Glue spirals of string onto the necklace pieces for relief decoration. Pierce holes with a skewer or a darning needle in the necklace pieces, headdress, and star as shown.

5

Cover the pieces with latex. Then paint the star and necklace pieces a shiny, Aztec gold. Use jade green for the headdress—the Aztecs loved jade.

6

When the headdress is dry, rub gold paint over the green with a cloth. Use a fine brush to paint extra details on all the pieces, then varnish.

7

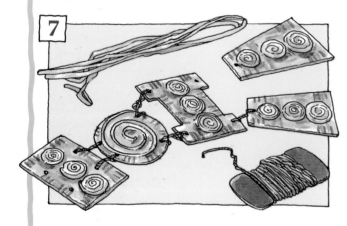

Tie the necklace pieces together with short lengths of sparkling gold string. Use gold raffia at the top to hang the necklace around your neck.

8

Glue brightly colored feathers to the top of your headdress. Use wire to attach the star firmly on top, hiding the glue. Twist the wire at the back.

9

Glue bright felt streamers to the inside of the head-dress, so they flop over the top. To finish, glue on gems, sequins, and coils of string.

SHOWING OFF

Forget about boring old boxes! Why not show the pieces you have made on a crazy jewelry cactus? You can buy scrap wood for the base from a hardware store.

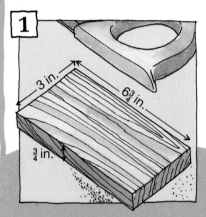

1

Ask an adult to saw a small block of wood (about 7 x 3 x ¾ inch) for a sturdy base.

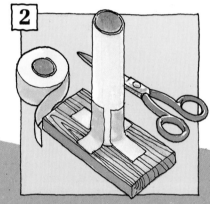

2

Use tape to attach a cardboard tube, such as a toilet-paper roll, to the base.

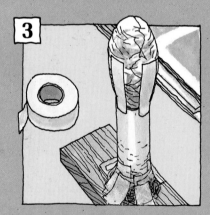

3

Crumple some paper, stuff it into the tube, then tape it in place. This is for attaching your branches.

4

Cut out the branches from cardboard. The two large ones have two halves, so cut out four of these.

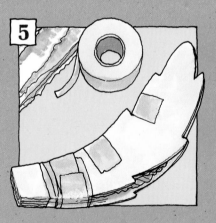

5

Stuff paper between the two halves of each large branch to pad it out. Hold the sides together with tape.

6

Tape all four branches to the cactus and cover everything with three layers of papier-mâché.

7

Give the cactus a latex base coat and then paint it bright green. Paint on yellow cactus spines, then varnish.

MORE IDEAS

By now you've probably realized that almost anything can be turned into jewelry. Here are a few more ideas you might like to try . . .

Wind some raffia around a cardboard bracelet. Sew embroidery thread in and out of the raffia, adding beads as you go.

Embroidery thread looks great braided. Tie the ends to a barrette, or knot them together to make a friendship bracelet. Add beads if you like.

For a choker, make a salt-dough heart with a hole in the middle. Use pink embroidery thread to sew the heart to a length of velvet ribbon. Glue on two Velcro squares for the fastening, or sew on snaps.

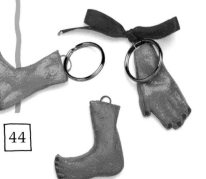

Use salt dough to make these cheerful key chain charms. Push in a paper clip before baking. After painting, slide it onto a key chain— you can buy them from craft stores.

STEP-BY-STEP
MAKING
KITES

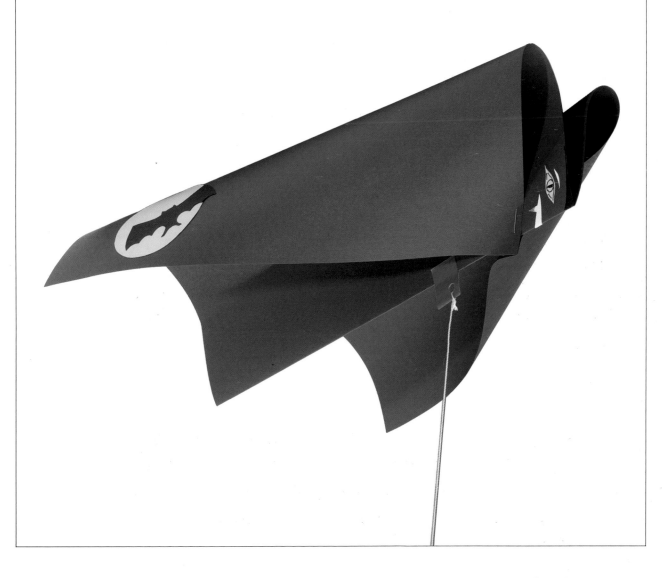

MAKING KITES

What You Need 48

Parts of a Kite 50

Making Kites 51

Tails 55

WHAT YOU NEED

To build most of the kites in this book, you will need to buy equipment from a specialist kite or hobby store. You will also need some simple household equipment and a generous working area — kite building takes up a lot of room.

Frame Materials

The *spars* or sticks that make the frame of a kite can be made from a variety of materials.

Bamboo is a traditional material and is still useful for smaller kites.

Wooden sticks can be bought in model and kite shops, as well as hardware stores.

Plastic rods are strong, light, and easily bent. Bigger sizes come in the form of hollow tubes, which reduce the weight.

More expensive, but strongest and lightest sticks of all, are those made from *carbon fiber*.

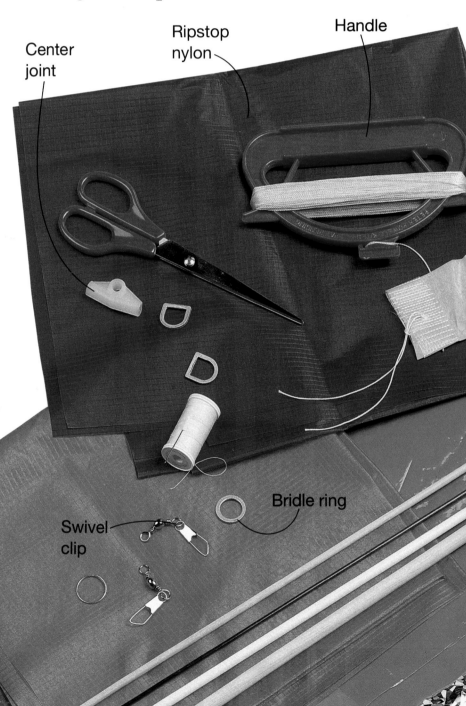

Center joint

Ripstop nylon

Handle

Swivel clip

Bridle ring

48

Sail Materials

The sail of a kite can be made from anything that is light and won't tear easily. Light-wind kites can even be made from *paper*. *Plastic* sheeting is probably the best choice for beginners — it is strong, waterproof, and can be repaired with tape. *Coated ripstop nylon* needs to be sewn rather than taped, but it is the first choice of the experienced kite builder.

Lines and Rings

String comes in many different weights, from thin thread for light kites to super-strong, tough enough to lift you off the ground! For your first kites, buy medium-strength string and a simple plastic handle. Later, you may prefer to use string mounted on a reel. Buy aluminum bridle rings, or use curtain rings. A swivel clip lets you add a spinning tail.

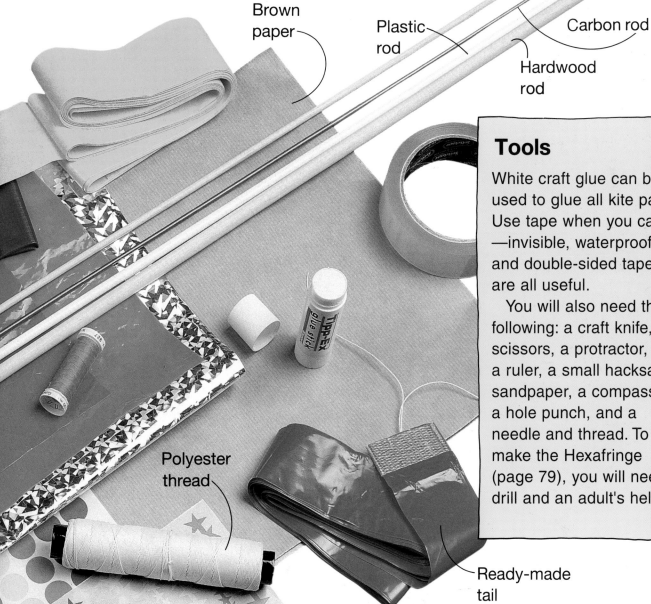

Brown paper

Plastic rod

Carbon rod

Hardwood rod

Polyester thread

Ready-made tail

Tools

White craft glue can be used to glue all kite parts. Use tape when you can —invisible, waterproof, and double-sided tape are all useful.

You will also need the following: a craft knife, scissors, a protractor, a ruler, a small hacksaw, sandpaper, a compass, a hole punch, and a needle and thread. To make the Hexafringe (page 79), you will need a drill and an adult's help.

49

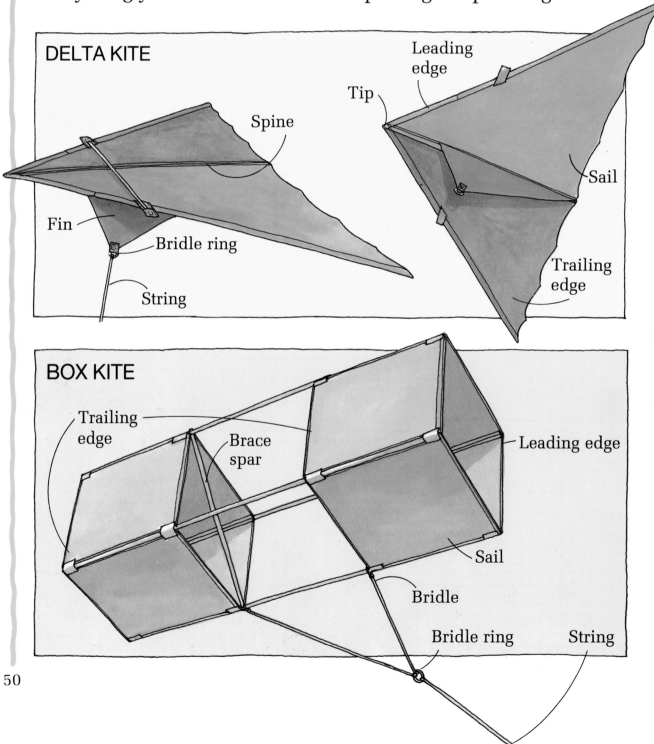

PARTS OF A KITE

Although the kites in this book all have different designs, the basic parts share the same name. These parts are shown in the diagrams below. On the following pages, you will find everything you need to know about putting the parts together.

DELTA KITE

Leading edge

Tip

Spine

Sail

Fin

Bridle ring

Trailing edge

String

BOX KITE

Trailing edge

Brace spar

Leading edge

Sail

Bridle

Bridle ring

String

MAKING KITES

Making kites isn't difficult. Follow the instructions carefully, and check your measurements at every stage. If you do, your kites should fly just as well as the ones that we built while making this book!

Making the Frame

To make the spars, cut the dowel, plastic, or carbon rods into lengths with a small hacksaw. Try to keep the sawing even and gradual — if you try to force the spars, they may snap. Use fine sandpaper to smooth the edges of the spar ends.

Joints

To join the spars, you can use strong twine, tape, or glue. For kites with angled sails (for example, the Superstunter on page 74), you will need to buy a metal or plastic bent center joint from a kite store. Plastic joints are rigid, but metal joints can be bent to fit the angle of your kite.

Joining Sails

To join plastic, paper, or cardboard, you can use tape. Overlap materials wherever possible, and tape both sides for extra strength. If you are using ripstop nylon, you should sew the pieces with a needle and thread. Overlap the edges by at least half an inch, and try to make the stitches small and neat. For extra strength, stitch two parallel lines, $\frac{1}{4}$ inch apart.

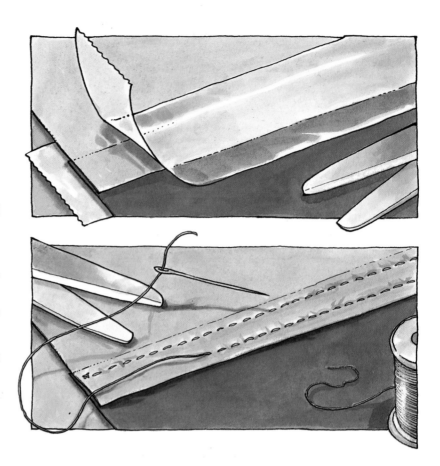

Making Pockets

The spars are kept in place by pockets at the tip, base, and top ends. They are quite simple to make.

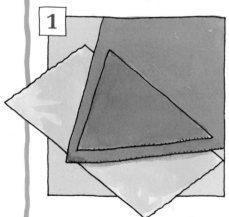

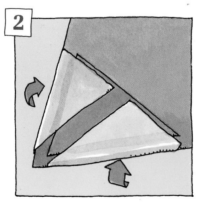

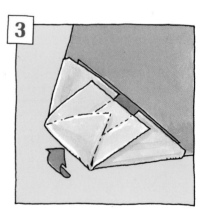

1

Taping Pockets:
Cut a triangle out of strong plastic to match the corner of the sail of the kite.

2

Use a strip of tape to attach the triangle to the corner of the sail to make a pocket.

3

Fold down the tip of the pocket to make a straight edge. Tape in place securely.

Sewing Pockets:

Cut a strip from nylon, $3\frac{1}{2}$ x 1 inch. Fold in half and sew as shown. Lay the pocket over the corner of the sail, so that it overlaps the corner. Sew it to the sail — the x-shaped stitching will add extra strength.

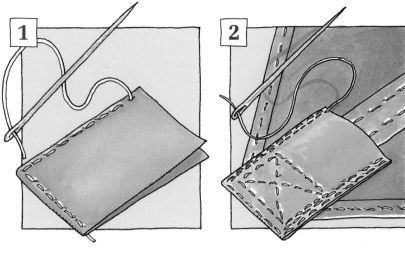

Bridle Ring Pocket:

The Delta kite on page 76 uses a bridle ring pocket. To make it, just follow the stages shown here.

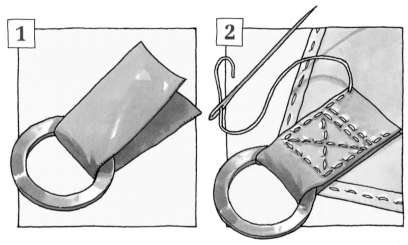

Below: The corner pockets and bridle ring pocket are sewn to ripstop nylon sails, using strong polyester thread.

Attaching Strings

When making kites, you will need to use two main strings. The *bridle* is tied to the kite at one end (using a bowline knot) and to a *bridle ring* at the other end (using a lark's head knot). The *string* is then tied to the bridle ring with a bowline knot. These two knots are shown below.

Lark's Head Knot

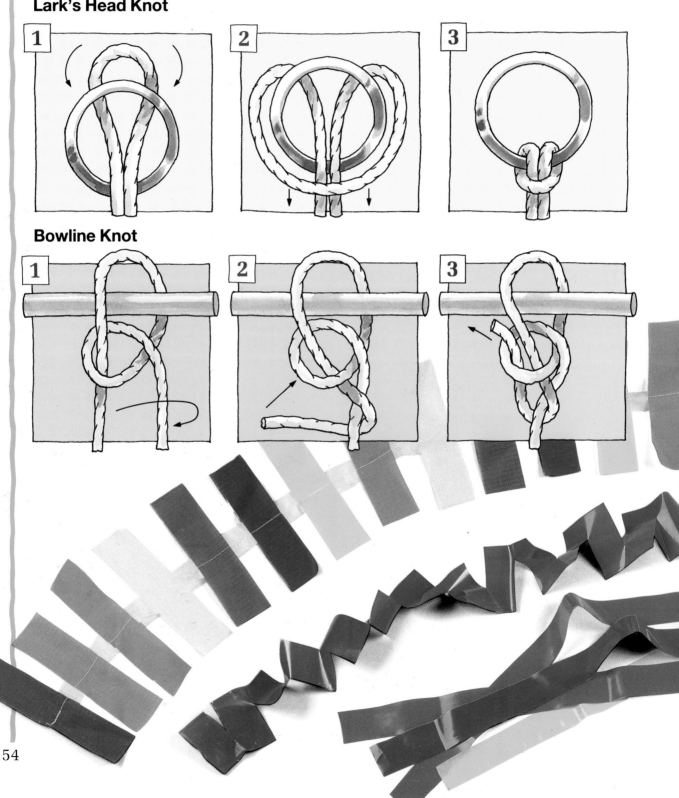

Bowline Knot

TAILS

Tails are not only colorful and attractive. They have a practical use, too. They make a kite more stable in the air and are essential for many designs, such as the Diamond Two-stick on page 66, and other kites with flat sails.

A simple ribbon tail can be made by cutting plastic or nylon into a long strip, 1 to 2 inches wide.

This tail catches more air than a ribbon. Simply cut notches down its entire length with scissors.

Tassel tails are made by joining a group of multi-colored ribbons at the base of the kite.

Streamer tails are fastened, evenly spaced, across the base of a flat kite.

A flat tail uses one single wide ribbon (see the Black Mamba on page 73).

DECORATIONS

For added interest, try making some of the decorations shown here. They add color and stability to the kite, and look spectacular in the air.

Spinning Helix

This kite looks hypnotically attractive as it spins round and round in the wind.

Using a plate as a guide, cut a large circle out of light cardboard or shiny Melinex.

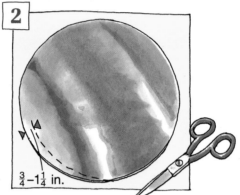

Mark a point $\frac{3}{4}$ to $1\frac{1}{4}$ inches from the edge. Make a slanted cut to form the end of the tail.

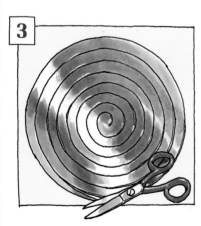

Keep cutting in a spiral until you reach the center. Keep the lines $\frac{3}{4}$ to $1\frac{1}{4}$ inches apart.

Attach the helix to the base of your kite, using a swivel clip (available from a kite shop).

Wind sock

This can be made from nylon, plastic, or
(as here) from shiny plastic wrapping paper.

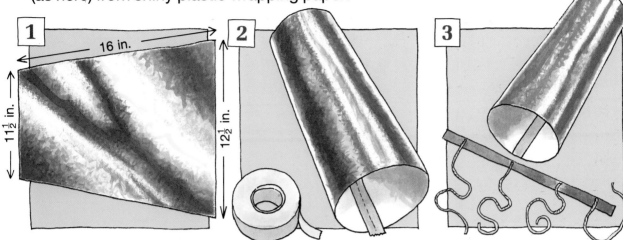

1 16 in. 11½ in.

2 12½ in.

3

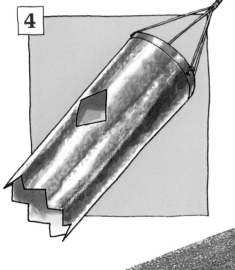

4

Cut out a rectangle of the paper, making the sides 16 x 12½ in. Cut as shown, so that the trailing edge measures 11½ in. across. Roll up into a tube, and tape

along the inside. Cut four pieces of string into 15-in. lengths, and cut a 13-in. piece of tape. Position the ends of the string along the sticky side, spacing the pieces

Cut the end of the wind sock into a pointed pattern. If you like, cut diamonds out of the sides, as shown.

equally as shown above. Roll the wider end of the wind sock carefully along the tape. Tie the loose ends of string together, and tie to the base of the kite.

Tailspinner

This tailspinner spins around in the wind, sending its ribbons flying through the air.

Making the Tailspinner

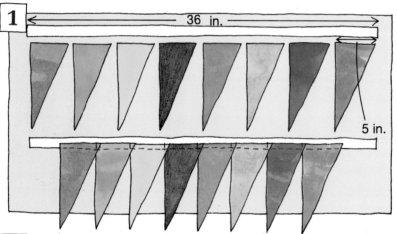

Cut eight triangles out of plastic or nylon. Make each triangle about 5 inches on the short end. Cut a band 1 yard in length from ripstop nylon. Sew on the triangles, overlapping each one by $\frac{1}{2}$ inch at the top.

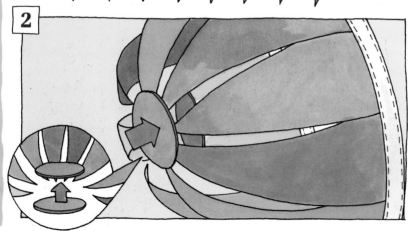

Cut two tail disks out of plastic or nylon. Use a compass to make sure they measure $1\frac{1}{4}$ inches across. Glue the tips of the triangles under the tips of one of the circles, then glue the second circle underneath the triangle tips.

58

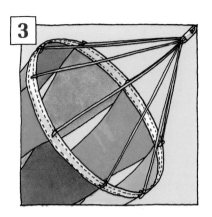

Cut eight pieces of kite string, each 10 inches long. Tape them to the band and tie the other ends to a swivel clip.

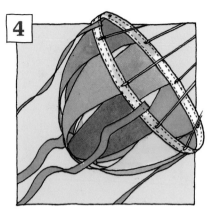

Tie or sew on four streamers made from bright pieces of plastic. These whirl around in a spiral.

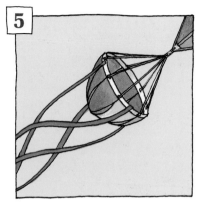

Attach the swivel clip to the base of the kite. Or, if you prefer, clip the tailspinner halfway up the kite string.

Climbing the line

When your kite is flying in the sky, what else can you do? Try slotting this little spinner up the line, and letting go. . .

Cut a 4-inch-diameter disk from stiff cardboard. Make a hole (about $\frac{1}{8}$ inch wide) through the center.

Use a compass to draw four $1\frac{1}{3}$ inch circles. Cut out half the circles, and bend up as shown. Cut the line A to B.

Cut a $2\frac{1}{3}$-inch length of plastic straw, and cut a lengthwise slit in it. Glue in the center of the disk at right angles, so that both cuts line up.

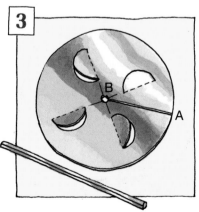

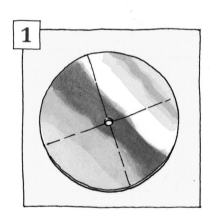

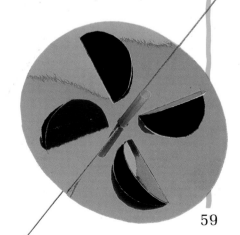

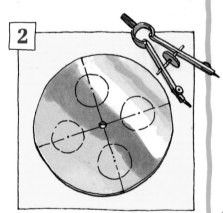

FLIGHT TESTING

The test flight is the moment of truth — have you built the kite well? Will it fly, or will it crash? Will it even get off the ground? Hopefully, it will soar like a bird — but you may need to adjust the balance first. Always choose open land to fly in, and don't try to fly the kite in very strong winds or when the air is still.

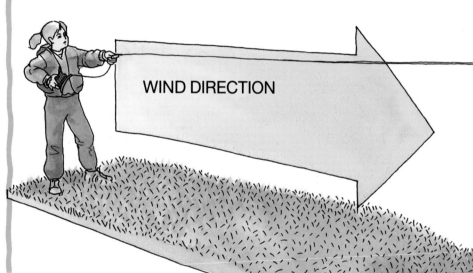

WIND DIRECTION

Launching is easier with two people. Unwind 20-30 feet of string and pull it taut. Make sure that your helper is facing into the wind. He or she should raise the kite into the air, with the kite facing the wind. Pull firmly on the string — the kite should soar up. If it doesn't, try walking backward or give a few sharp tugs on the kite string.

Flight Safety

* Keep away from electricity wires, trees, and houses.

* Don't fly kites near airfields, or at heights which may get in the way of aircraft.

* Use leather gloves if it is very windy. The string can burn the hands if it unwinds suddenly.

* Don't fly in stormy weather. Lightning could strike the kite and kill you.

* Don't launch the kite if people or animals are walking past.

Adjusting the Balance

A kite that flies perfectly one day may fly badly the next time you take it out — this may be due to a change in wind conditions. Try moving the bridle ring.

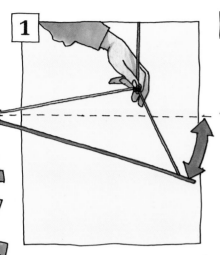

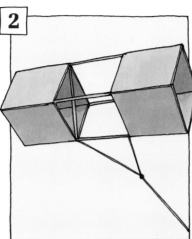

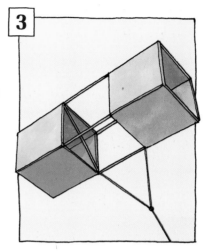

Before flight, hold the kite by the bridle ring. Adjust the ring so that the kite hangs at 20-30° into the wind.

Moving the bridle forward makes the kite fly higher, at a flat angle to the wind. This is good for smooth winds.

Moving the bridle back makes the kite fly at a steeper angle. Use in medium to gusty wind conditions.

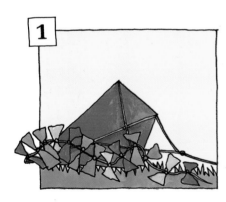

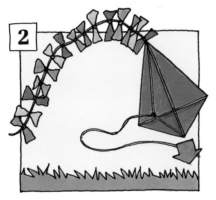

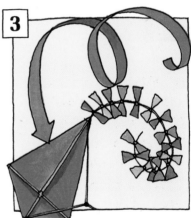

Trouble Shooting

Kite fails to rise: not enough wind, bridle too short, or tail too long.

Kite flies, then crashes: bridle may need to be shortened.

Kite spins or wobbles: add more tail.

Landing your kite

To land your kite, wind in the string on your reel. If the wind is quite strong, try pulling the string in hand over hand until the kite comes down.

DRACULA'S CLOAK

All kinds of simple kites can be made out of paper. Dracula's Cloak can be made out of plain white paper, but it looks much more sinister in purple or black. It flies well in a gentle breeze.

Instead of painting your kite, try cutting shapes out of colored paper and gluing them on the surface with white paste.

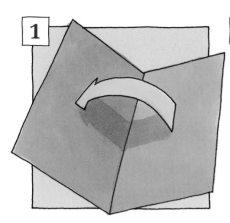

1

Fold a $11\frac{1}{2}$ x $16\frac{1}{2}$-inch sheet of typing-weight paper carefully across the middle as shown above.

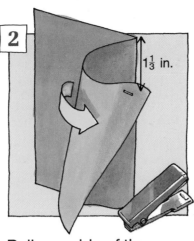

2

$1\frac{1}{3}$ in.

Pull one side of the sheet around in a curve. Staple it against the center fold, $1\frac{1}{3}$ inches from the tip.

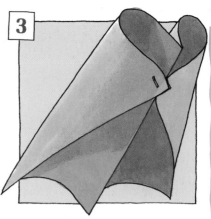

3

Repeat on the other side. Make sure the corners slightly overlap the center fold, as shown above.

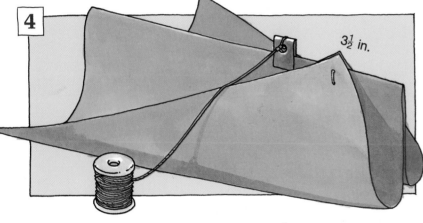

4

$3\frac{1}{2}$ in.

5

The Dracula's Cloak kite doesn't need a bridle ring. Just cut a square piece of thick tape and press it on the center

fold, $3\frac{1}{2}$ inches from the tip. Make a hole in the tape as shown in the picture with a hole punch or a pair of scissors.

Use lightweight thread to fly the Cloak. It will rise in the lightest breeze and hover menacingly above you!

Dracula's Cloak takes on a bloodthirsty look if you paint some talons, fangs, and a leering face on it. Use felt-tip pens on white paper, and poster paints on colored paper.

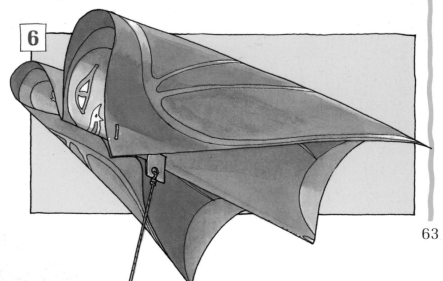

6

TWIN-FIN SKYSLED

Another good flyer in light winds, this kite can be made out of paper or plastic. The one shown here is a good pocket-sized kite, but it could also be made on a larger scale.

Colored tape was used to decorate this Twin-Fin. You could also use bright poster paint.

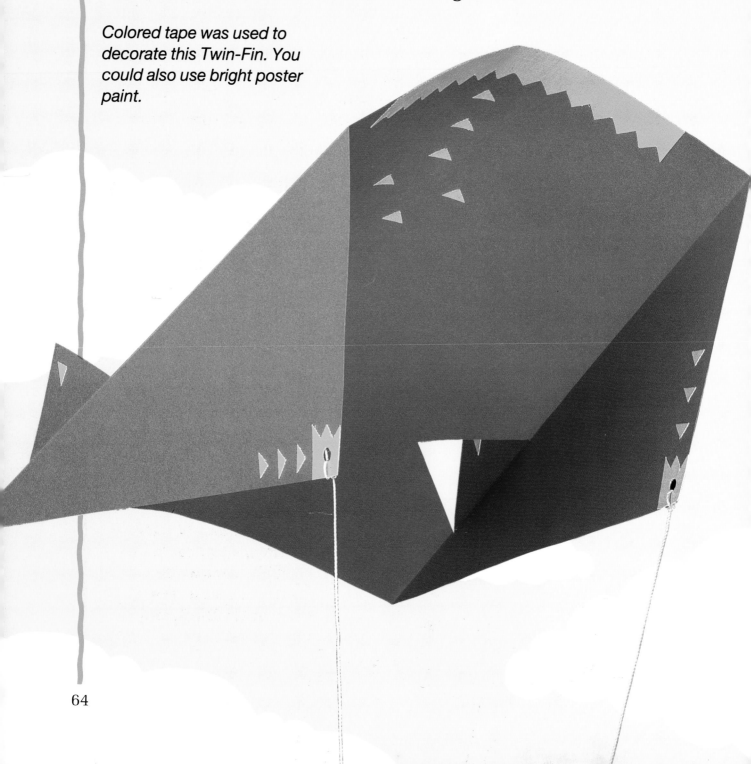

64

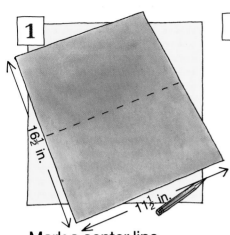

1 Mark a center line down the middle of a piece of paper $11\frac{1}{2}$ x $16\frac{1}{2}$ inches. Do not fold the sheet, as this will spoil flight performance.

16½ in.

11½ in.

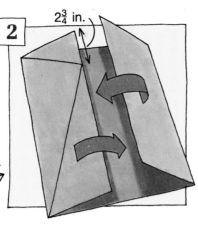

2 Fold both ends in to the center line. Cut the sides in the triangle pattern shown — the tips should be $2\frac{3}{4}$ inches from the end of the kite.

$2\frac{3}{4}$ in.

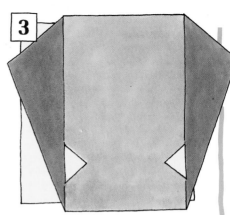

3 Cut out the two twin-fin stabilizers. Heavy paper fins can be folded up. Plastic ones will flop until they are blown by the wind.

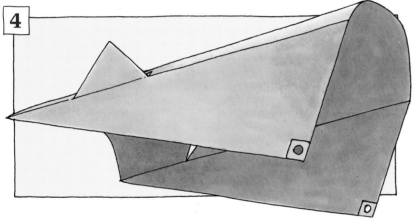

4 Strengthen the corners to take the strain of the bridle. It is simplest to use strong tape and to make the holes with a hole punch.

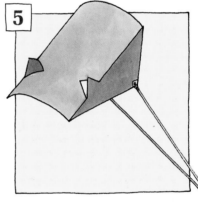

5 Tie on a long bridle, two to three times the length of the kite. Start with 27 inches, and adjust if necessary.

Use Melinex or shiny wrapping paper to make a kite which dazzles like an alien spacecraft in the sky!

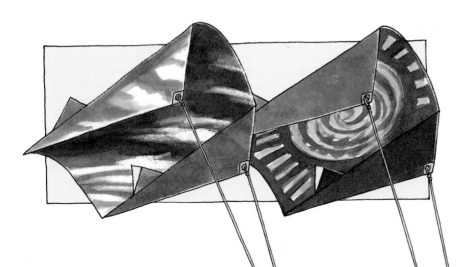

65

DIAMOND TWO-STICK

The Diamond Two-stick is a classic kite design. The one shown here has two bridle rings — use the top ring in light winds, the bottom one for stronger conditions. Add a longer tail if the kite wobbles in flight.

1

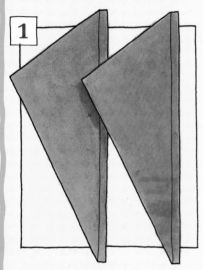

Cut two triangles out of plastic sheeting or rip-stop nylon. Make them the same size, and allow an extra $\frac{3}{8}$-inch overlap on the spine edge.

2

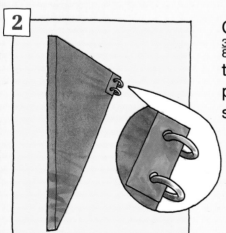

3

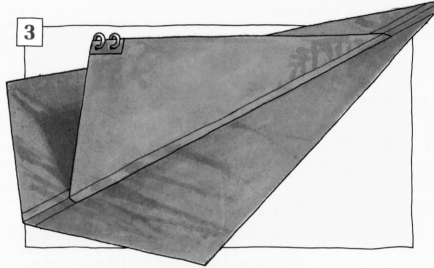

Sew or tape the two sails together. Join them along their longest sides, as shown above. Sew or tape on the fin, positioning it $3\frac{1}{2}$ inches from the tip of the kite.

Cut out a fin, allowing $\frac{3}{8}$-inch overlap. Cover the corner with tape, punch two holes, and slip on two split rings.

4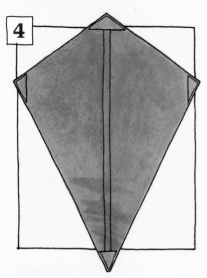

5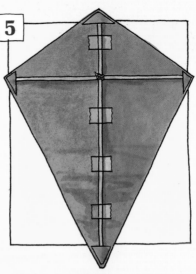

6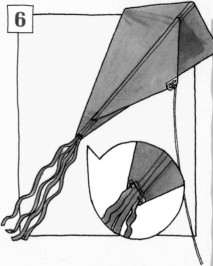

Tape or sew triangular pockets to the tip, base, and sail ends. They need to be very strong, so use thicker material than the sail fabric.

Cut two pieces of dowel ($\frac{1}{4}$-inch diameter) to fit the kite. Slide in place and tie them where they cross. Tape the spine stick to the sail, or sew cotton tape to the sail and tie to the spars.

Cut four plastic tails, each measuring 2 inches wide x 6 feet long. Attach two of them to the base of the kite with a safety pin. Add the other two tails if the kite isn't a stable flyer. Attach the kite string to the top or bottom bridle ring, depending on wind conditions.

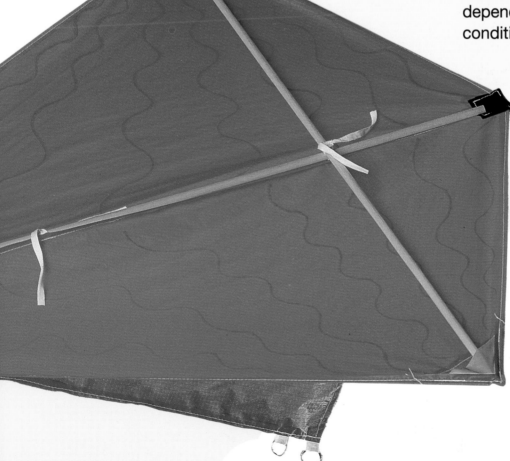

THE RINGWING

This Ringwing was made out of thin cardboard and $\frac{1}{4}$-inch diameter carbon fiber rod. It flies well, but needs a strong wind for a good liftoff.

1

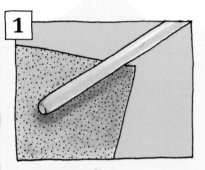

Cut a 36-inch-long piece of dowel or carbon fiber rod. Smooth the ends with sandpaper.

2

10 in.

27 in.

Cut two pieces of thin cardboard, each 10 x 27 inches. Press double-sided tape on one end of each sheet.

3

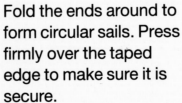

Fold the ends around to form circular sails. Press firmly over the taped edge to make sure it is secure.

4

Use white glue to attach each sail to the spar, and tape them in place. Try to make sure the sails are perfectly straight.

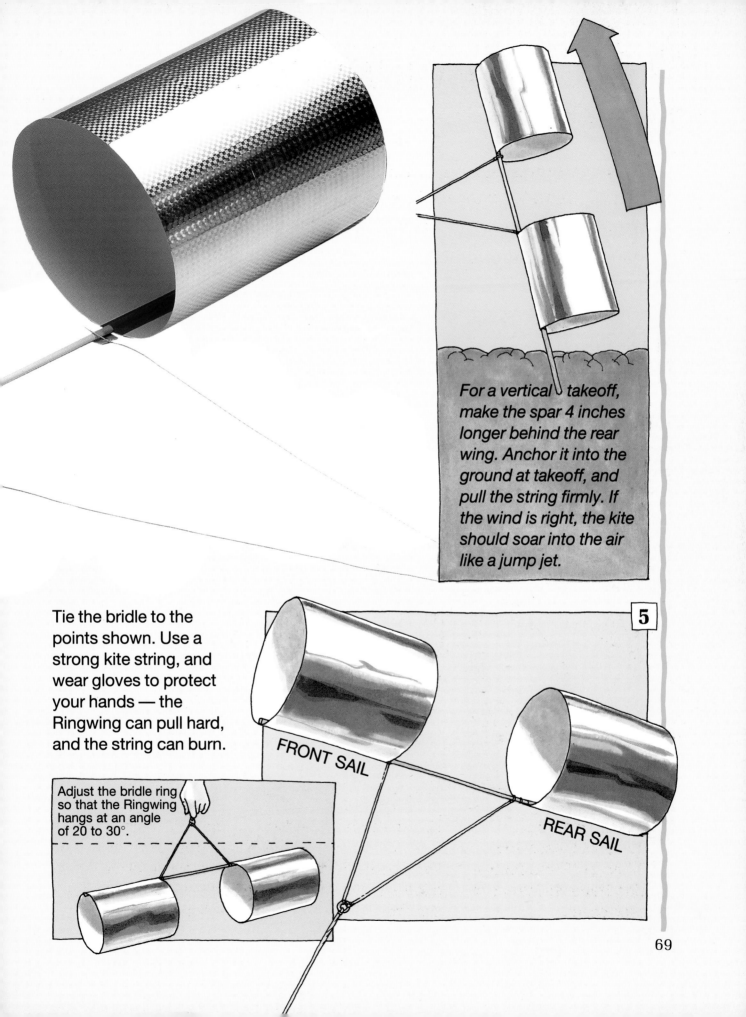

For a vertical takeoff, make the spar 4 inches longer behind the rear wing. Anchor it into the ground at takeoff, and pull the string firmly. If the wind is right, the kite should soar into the air like a jump jet.

Tie the bridle to the points shown. Use a strong kite string, and wear gloves to protect your hands — the Ringwing can pull hard, and the string can burn.

Adjust the bridle ring so that the Ringwing hangs at an angle of 20 to 30°.

FRONT SAIL

REAR SAIL

5

BOX KITE

The sails of this box kite are made from acoustic tiles. They can be bought in hardware stores, and come in standard sizes — usually 12 inches square. The frame is made from $\frac{1}{4}$-inch diameter wooden dowel.

1 Lay four tiles in a straight line on a flat surface. Make sure that the angled edges are face down. Tape the tiles together at the edges. Then fold them into a box shape, and tape together on the inside, as shown below.

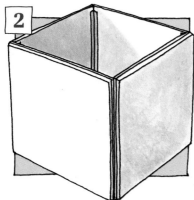

2 Make another sail the same way, making sure that the edges are evenly taped.

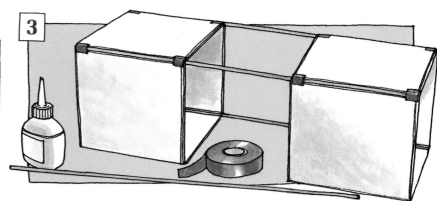

3 Cut the dowels into four spars, each 36 inches long. Glue to the sails with white glue, and hold in place with tape. The spars should fit into the angled corners of the cubes as shown.

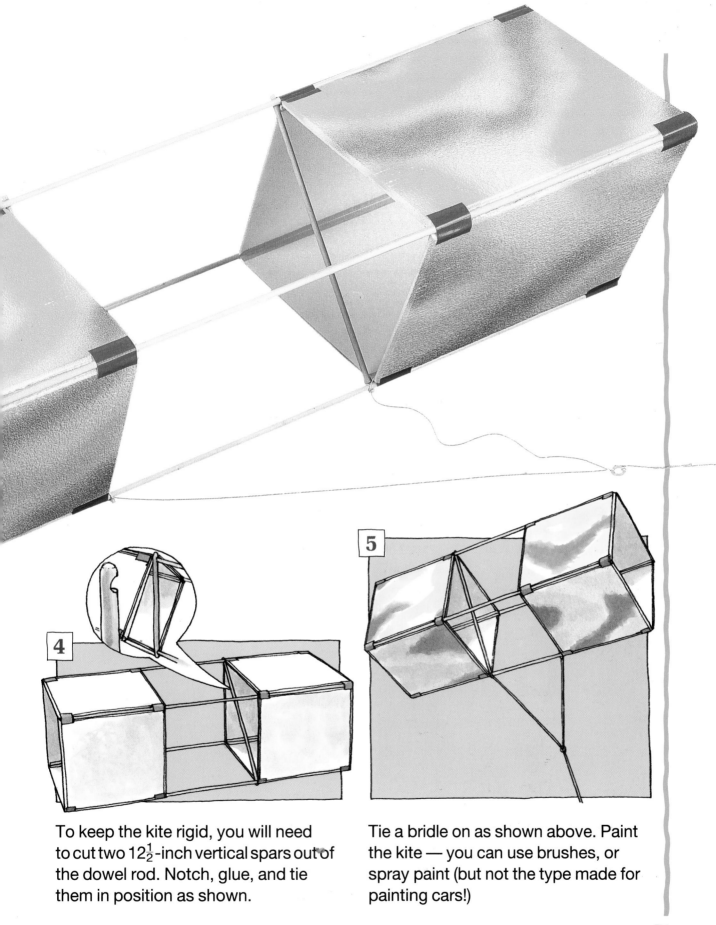

4 To keep the kite rigid, you will need to cut two $12\frac{1}{2}$-inch vertical spars out of the dowel rod. Notch, glue, and tie them in position as shown.

5 Tie a bridle on as shown above. Paint the kite — you can use brushes, or spray paint (but not the type made for painting cars!)

THE BLACK MAMBA

The sight of the Mamba slithering across the sky is enough to send a shiver down the strongest spine — yet it's little more than a cleverly sliced plastic garbage bag.

1

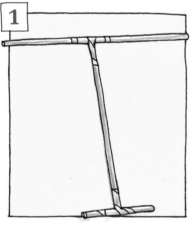

Cut three lengths of $\frac{1}{8}$-inch diameter plastic rod to make a T-shape, as shown in the diagram. Fasten the three rods together with tape.

2

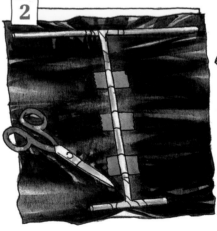

Cut open a black plastic garbage bag, and lay the frame on top. Tape the spine and base. Trim the plastic, leaving $\frac{3}{4}$ inch at the top and bottom.

3

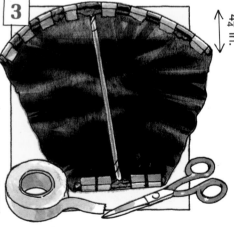

$4\frac{1}{4}$ in.

Bend down the top rod so that the ends are $4\frac{1}{4}$ inches below the tip. Tape the plastic securely, and trim the sides as shown.

Cut sinister features from colored paper or plastic and glue them on the Mamba's face.

4 Tape the edges — this adds strength to the kite and prevents it from ripping in strong winds, or when it is coming in to land.

5 Cut the rest of the bag into 6-inch-wide strips. Tape them together to make a long tail, and cut the end into a point. Tape the flat edge to the base of the kite. Make two holes as shown, and tie on a bridle — adjust it if you need to improve the Mamba's flight.

THE SUPERSTUNTER

Take command of the air with this twin-line kite! The two lines let you climb, dive, spin, and soar, but be warned — the Superstunter is a nervous flyer, and the slightest mistake will send it hurtling to the ground.

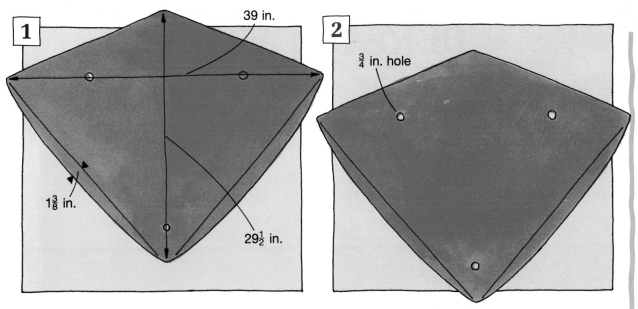

1 39 in. 1⅜ in. 29½ in.

Draw this sail plan on a large sheet of paper to the sizes shown. Cut out, and pin to a sheet of plastic. Cut out the plastic sail.

2 ¾ in. hole

Make three holes, ¾ inch across, for the bridle. Then tape a plastic pocket (buy these from a kite store, or make your own) into each corner.

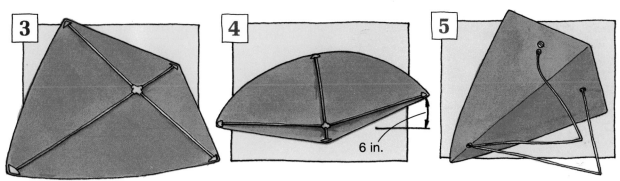

3

Cut four pieces of ¼-inch dowel to fit the sail. Put into a metal joint, and slip the ends into the pockets.

4 6 in.

To make the angled wing, keep one wing flat on your work surface and bend up the other wing.

5

Two bridles are used for this kite. Tie them to the spars through the holes, as shown above.

Tie on the bridle rings, and tie to two separate kite strings. Make tails by cutting old plastic bags into streamers and taping them to the base of the kite.

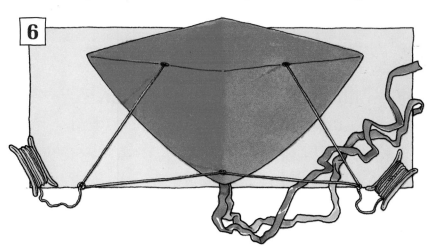

6

DELTA STAR

Use adhesive shapes as a quick way of decorating your Delta.

This classic design flies in light winds and is very stable. It can be made from plastic and tape or sewn in ripstop nylon like the one shown here. Add long pennants and streamers for extra interest.

76

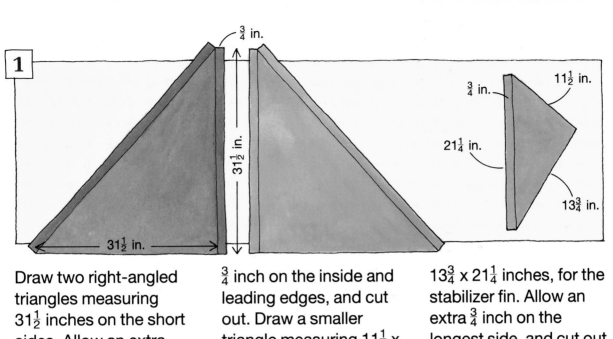

1 Draw two right-angled triangles measuring 31½ inches on the short sides. Allow an extra ¾ inch on the inside and leading edges, and cut out. Draw a smaller triangle measuring 11½ x 13¾ x 21¼ inches, for the stabilizer fin. Allow an extra ¾ inch on the longest side, and cut out.

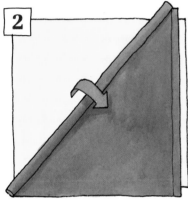

2 Fold the leading edges over, and sew to make a pocket for the wing spars.

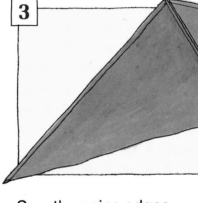

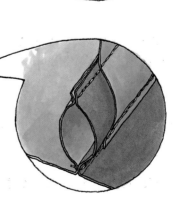

3 Sew the spine edges together with a double seam casing to make a casing for the spine spar.

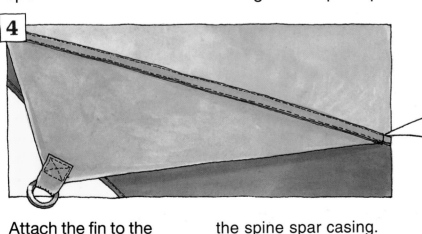

4 Attach the fin to the spine as shown by sewing down the side of the spine spar casing. Sew a bridle ring pocket to the fin (see page 53).

5

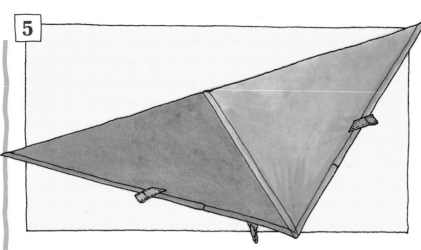

Make two pockets for the cross-brace spar. Sew the pockets to the leading edges, as shown

on page 53. Make sure that the pockets are positioned 20 inches from the tip of the kite.

6

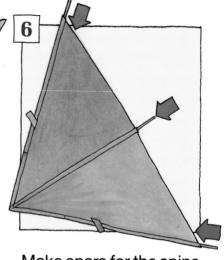

Make spars for the spine and leading edges from $\frac{1}{4}$-inch dowel cut into 8-inch lengths.

7

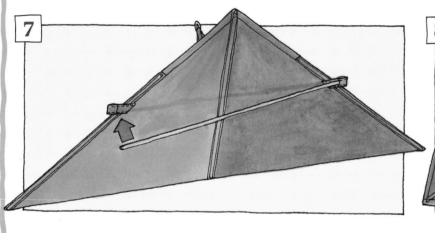

Cut another piece of $\frac{1}{4}$-inch dowel $31\frac{1}{2}$ inches long. This is the cross-brace spar. Slip the ends

of the spar into the two pockets you have attached to the leading edges of the kite.

8

If you like, cut a scalloped edge along the base of the Delta, as shown above.

Decorate the Delta with adhesive stars, and attach tails to the base. You could also add a tailspinner (page 58), or even tie on a banner with a message!

9

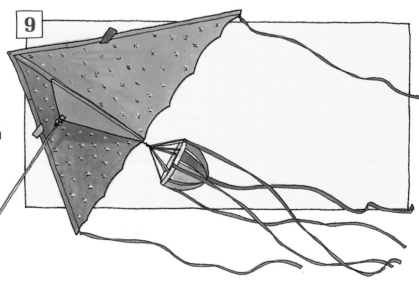

HEXAFRINGE

The design for this six-sided kite comes from Greece, a land of sea and sunshine. On a sunny day, the kite's many-colored fringe and long tail make it one of the prettiest you are likely to see. To make it, you will need to do some drilling — ask an adult to help you.

1

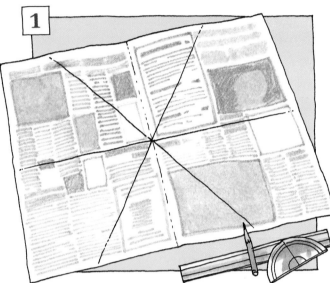

Draw the pattern shown above on a large sheet of newspaper. Use a protractor to make each angle measure 60°.

Cut $\frac{1}{4}$-inch-square wooden sticks into three $31\frac{1}{2}$-inch lengths. Smooth the ends with sandpaper. Using a very small drill bit, make a hole $\frac{1}{8}$ inch from the end of each stick.

Tape the sticks to the pattern, one on top of the other. Make sure that the holes are on the sides. Then firmly tie the sticks in the middle with twine. Remove the pattern.

2

3

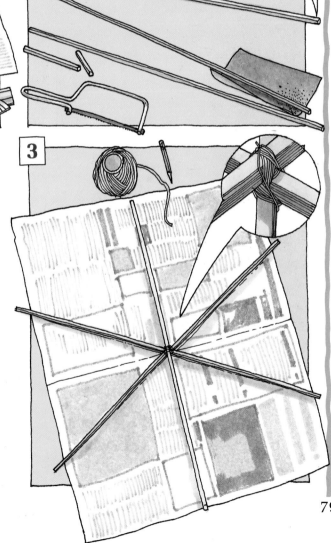

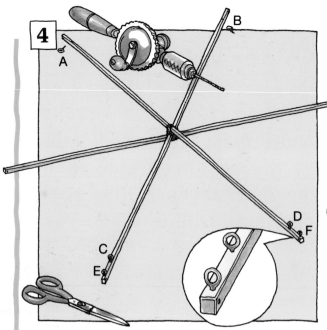

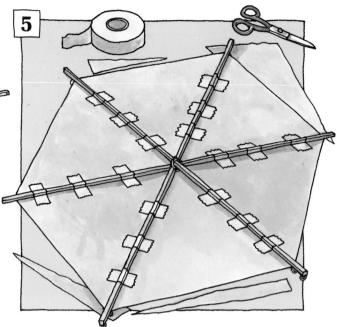

4 Drill four more holes, A, B, C, and D, 2 inches from the end of the spars. These are for the bridles. Finally, drill holes E and F, $\frac{3}{8}$ inch from the ends. These are for the tail. Screw eyehooks into all these six holes.

5 Tape the spars firmly to a large sheet of brown wrapping paper with the eyehooks pointing down. Cut the paper into a hexagonal sail, as shown — the spars must be 2 inches longer than the sail.

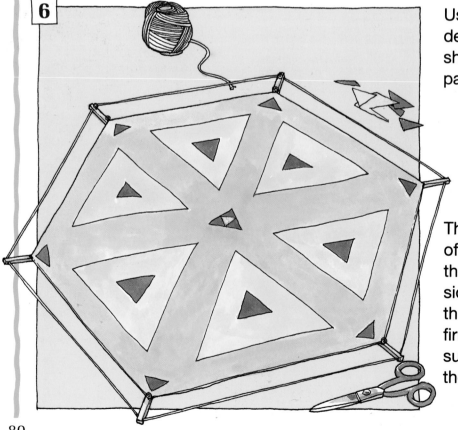

6 Use poster paint to decorate the sail, or glue shapes cut from colored paper.

Thread a long length of fishing line or strong thread through the side holes at the end of the spars, and tie firmly. This line supports the fringe of the kite.

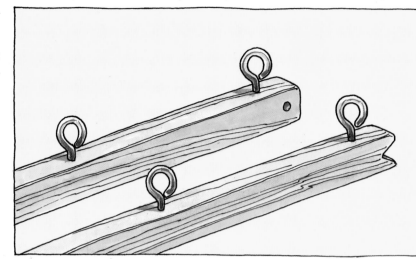

Holes and Notches

As an alternative to drilling holes for the fringe, you could try cutting V-shaped notches at the end of each spar with a craft knife. As with drilling, always ask an adult to help you.

7

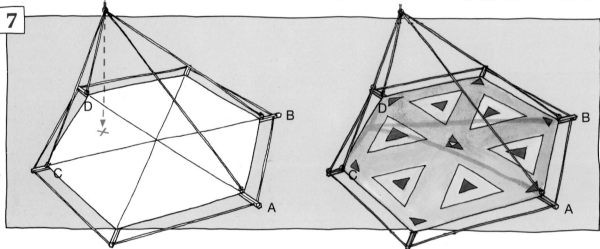

Cut four pieces of kite string for the bridle. Tie one end of a piece of string to each eyehook (marked A, B, C, and D). Then tie the free ends to a bridle ring. You will need to adjust the length of each bridle line, so that when the kite is held by the bridle ring, the four lines meet at a point directly above and in the middle of points C and D (see the diagram above).

Cut two more pieces of string, and tie them to the eyehooks E and F. Tie them together so that the lines run parallel to the edges of the kite.

8

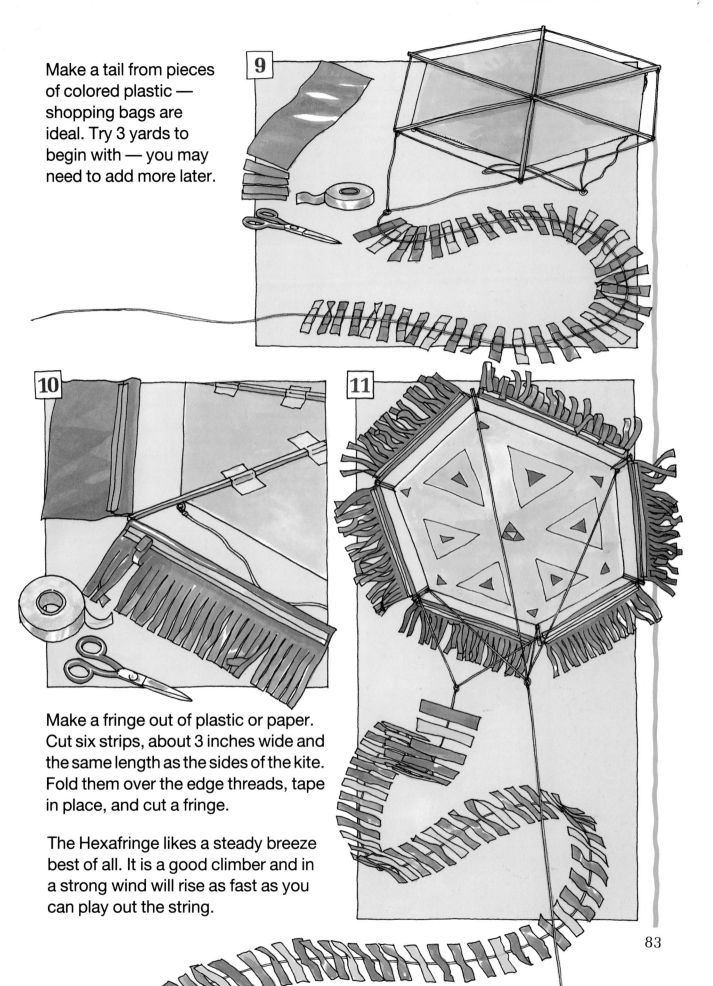

9 Make a tail from pieces of colored plastic — shopping bags are ideal. Try 3 yards to begin with — you may need to add more later.

10 Make a fringe out of plastic or paper. Cut six strips, about 3 inches wide and the same length as the sides of the kite. Fold them over the edge threads, tape in place, and cut a fringe.

The Hexafringe likes a steady breeze best of all. It is a good climber and in a strong wind will rise as fast as you can play out the string.

11

MORE IDEAS

Once you feel confident about making kites, you might like to try designing your own. In the meantime, here are a few more ideas for you to consider....

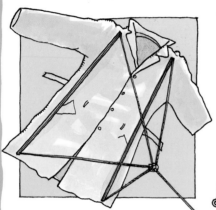

All you need is a thin plastic raincoat (the kind that folds into a pocket), and two wooden spars!

Based on ancient Chinese designs, this flying fish is little more than a decorated wind sock.

Tie balloons to the ends of poles, and use stunt kites to try to burst them. It's harder than you might think.

This tiny kite is only 1 inch across, but it can fly in front of a mini fan. Use very light sail material.

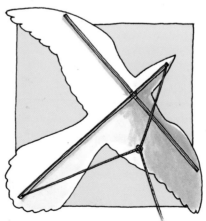

Kites in the shape of birds are fun. A prehistoric version could be made in the shape of a pterosaur.

Flying a stack of matching kites is a popular sport. The stable Delta kite is well suited to stacking.

STEP-BY-STEP
MAKING
CARDS

MAKING CARDS

WHAT YOU NEED

To make the cards in this book, collect together a basic kit like the one shown here. Some of the projects require a few extra bits and pieces—check by reading through the step-by-step instructions before you begin.

Glue

The Basics

The main thing you'll need is a supply of thin cardboard. Heavy paper can also work well. If you use thin paper, fold each sheet in half to double the thickness—otherwise they'll be too floppy to stand up!

Colored tissue, crepe, wrapping paper, old magazines, and wallpaper can all be used to decorate your cards.

Scissors

Felt-tip pens

Dried beans and lentils

Foam block

Square

Tools of the Trade

You'll need a pair of scissors, a square, a craft knife, a metal ruler, paintbrushes, pencils, and a cutting board to protect your table—a big piece of cardboard, wood, or Formica is ideal.

Always handle craft knives very carefully, and only use them when an adult is around to help.

Paints and Glue

For sticking paper and cardboard together, use ordinary white glue or paper paste.

Most of the cards in this book were decorated by cutting shapes out of paper and gluing them to the design. You could also color your cards with paints or felt-tip pens.

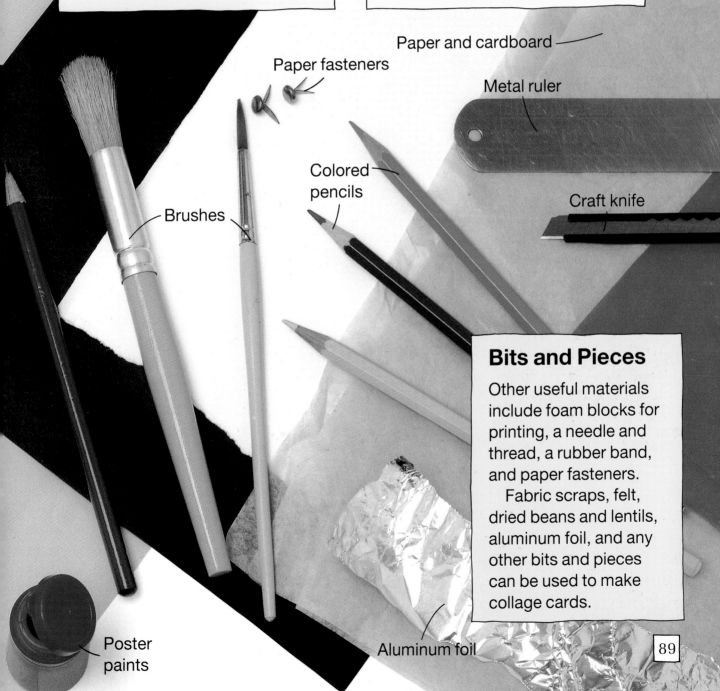

Paper and cardboard

Paper fasteners

Metal ruler

Colored pencils

Craft knife

Brushes

Bits and Pieces

Other useful materials include foam blocks for printing, a needle and thread, a rubber band, and paper fasteners.

Fabric scraps, felt, dried beans and lentils, aluminum foil, and any other bits and pieces can be used to make collage cards.

Poster paints

Aluminum foil

89

HINTS AND TIPS

The cards in this book are all easy to make—they're also a lot more fun to send than ones you've bought from a store! Just take your time, and follow all the instructions carefully. Before you start, read the tips below.

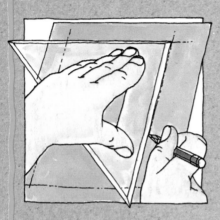

Measuring

It's best to use a square rather than a ruler when you're measuring your cards. If you use the right-angled edges to help you draw the corners, your cards will look very professional.

Folding

Folding cardboard is easier if you *score* it first. Measure and draw the fold line using a ruler and a pencil. Then press the nib of an empty ballpoint pen along the line, using a metal ruler as a guide.

Illustrating

To illustrate your cards, you could simply paint a design on the front. Or, cut shapes from colored paper and glue them down. You can even make collage cards, using all kinds of bits and pieces.

The pictures on the right show three different ways of illustrating the same design. Each illustration was done on a separate piece of cardboard, then cut and glued onto a piece of folded cardboard. This is called "mounting."

Painted card

Collage card,
made with felt,
beans, and seeds

Card decorated
with paper
shapes

91

PRINTING CARDS

Use small shapes to print borders. They are also a good way to build up pictures—for example, a simple oval shape was repeated to make the petals of the sunflower opposite.

1

Draw a simple shape onto a piece of thick Styrofoam using a felt-tip pen. Cut the shape out carefully with a craft knife.

2

Cut several squares from thin cardboard or construction paper, each a little smaller than the folded cards you have already prepared.

Printing is a quick way to make a big batch of cards—at Christmas, for example, or when you want to invite a lot of friends to a party. Before you start printing, cut out all the cards you need. Fold them in half and put them to one side.

3 Pour some poster paint into a saucer. Dip the printing shape into the paint and press it firmly onto one of the squares.

4 Keep dipping and printing until you have enough pictures. When they're dry, mount them onto the front of the folded cards.

MAKING ENVELOPES

Your cards will look extra special if you send them in your own homemade envelopes! The instructions given here will work for any size. Try printing the backs and borders with brightly colored paints (see pages 92–93) and sealing the flaps with glue or stickers.

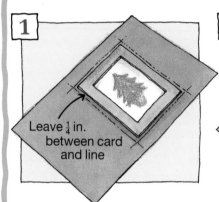

1

Leave ¼ in. between card and line

Lay your folded card on a big sheet of colored paper. Draw around it, making the line ¼ inch wider on all sides.

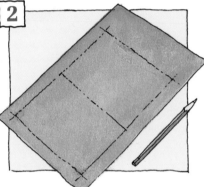

2

Draw another rectangle under the first one. It should be exactly the same width, but about ¼ inch shorter.

Why send plain envelopes when printed ones look so terrific?

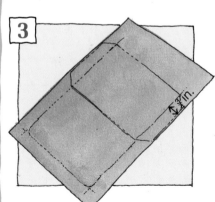

3

¾ in.

Draw curves inside the bottom two corners. Add two ¾-inch flaps at each side of the top rectangle, as shown.

4 | 2 in.

Draw a triangle at the top, making it at least 2 inches deep so that it overlaps the bottom rectangle when folded.

5 | Glue flaps

Cut out the shape with a craft knife. Fold all the lines inward, and glue the bottom rectangle over the side flaps.

BIRTHDAY SHAPES

Here are some very simple cards that just need a little folding and cutting. The colorful numbers would make great birthday cards for friends, brothers, or sisters—or how about making the leaping dolphin for an animal-loving mom or dad?

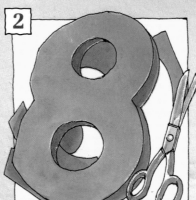

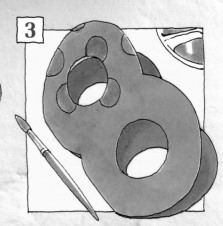

Number Cards

Draw a number onto a piece of folded cardboard. One side must touch the fold.

Cut out the number, making sure you don't cut through the folded part of the design.

Paint the card, or decorate it by gluing down shapes cut from colored paper.

4 Draw a triangle at the top, making it at least 2 inches deep so that it overlaps the bottom rectangle when folded.

2 in.

5 Cut out the shape with a craft knife. Fold all the lines inward, and glue the bottom rectangle over the side flaps.

Glue flaps

BIRTHDAY SHAPES

Here are some very simple cards that just need a little folding and cutting. The colorful numbers would make great birthday cards for friends, brothers, or sisters—or how about making the leaping dolphin for an animal-loving mom or dad?

1

Folded edge

2

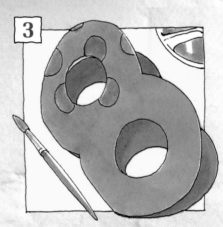

3

Number Cards

Draw a number onto a piece of folded card-board. One side must touch the fold.

Cut out the number, making sure you don't cut through the folded part of the design.

Paint the card, or decorate it by gluing down shapes cut from colored paper.

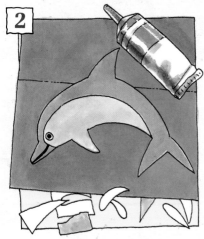

Stand-ups

Cut out a rectangle from cardboard and lightly pencil a line across the middle.

Draw a design with the top part just above the middle line. Color with paints or paper collage.

Cut around the top part with a craft knife. Then score along the line and fold backward.

The train was made in the same way as the number cards, but the folded edge is at the top, not at the side.

The ark and dolphin both have a simple stand-up shape that can easily be cut out with a craft knife.

SURPRISE!

Always keep the main picture of a surprise card hidden—just hint at what's underneath, as we've done here with the tip of the tiger's ears!

1

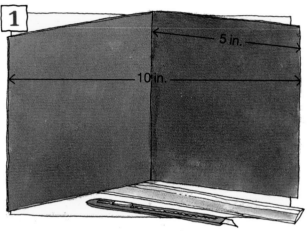

Measure a 10 x 5-inch rectangle onto a piece of green cardboard and cut it out. Score a line down the middle and fold the card in half.

2

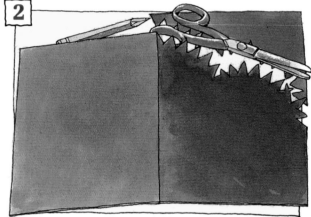

Draw a simple bush shape on the front of the card, as shown in the picture. Cut along this line, using a craft knife or scissors.

3

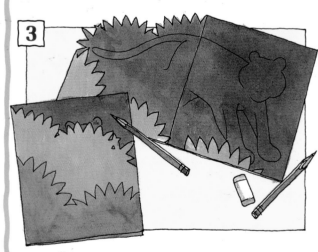

Close the card and lightly sketch the tip of the tiger's ears on the inside, using a pencil. Open the card again, and draw the rest of the tiger's body.

4

Use paints or pieces of colored paper to decorate the inside and outside of the card. Write your message on the back.

Secret Message

Cut a dog's body out of colored paper and glue it to the front of a folded piece of cardboard. Draw and cut out the dog's head, and glue just the top part to the card.

Make a tiny envelope (pages 94–95), tuck in a secret message, and stick it under the dog's chin!

PUZZLE CARDS

The pictures on these cards are magically revealed when the pieces are put in the right order or when the dots are joined together!

1

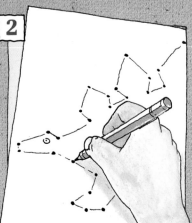

2

Dot-to-Dot

Lightly draw a simple design onto a piece of paper, using a pencil.

Use a felt-tip pen to mark clear dots along the pencil line.

3

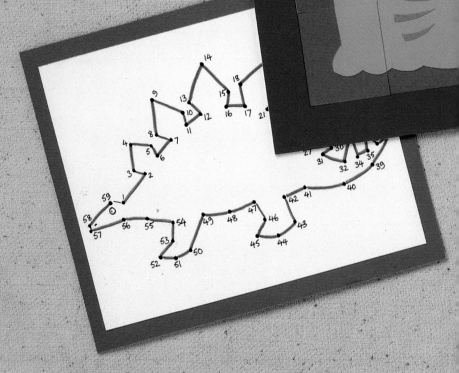

Number the dots in the correct order. Erase the pencil marks and mount the picture onto a card.

Jigsaw Card

1 Draw a rectangle measuring 7 x 6 inches onto a piece of cardboard. Cut it out.

6 in.

7 in.

2 Draw a border ¾ inch inside the edge of the cardboard. Cut along border to make a frame.

¾ in.

3 Place the frame on another piece of cardboard. Draw along the inside with a pencil, and cut this out.

4 Turn this piece of cardboard into a picture using paints or paper collage, then cut it into simple jigsaw pieces.

5 Fold a 12 x 7-inch piece of cardboard in half and glue the frame to the front. Send in an envelope, along with the jigsaw pieces.

101

POP-UP CARDS

These cards look terrific, and they're easy to make when you know how! You can change the picture to suit any kind of theme—just follow all the measurements given here.

1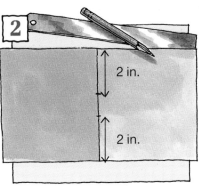

Take two pieces of thin cardboard, each 12 x 6 inches. Score and fold both pieces of cardboard down the middle.

2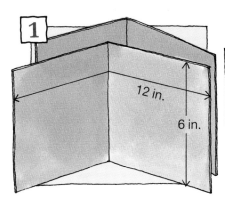

On one of the pieces, measure 2 inches along the fold from either edge, and mark the two points with a pencil.

3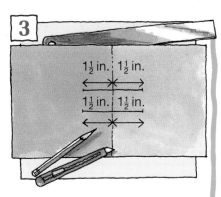

Draw a 3-inch line through each of these points (1½ inches on either side of the fold). Cut along both lines.

4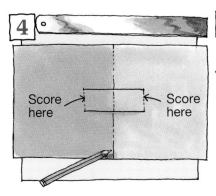

Now lightly score two lines between the cut lines, as shown.

5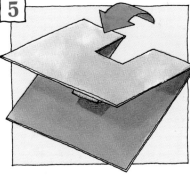

Close and open the card, making the center strip fold inward.

6

Decorate the background with paints or paper collage.

7

On a new piece of cardboard, draw a pop-up shape that will fit inside the card.

8

Cut out and decorate the pop-up shape. Glue it to the lower half of the center strip, as shown.

9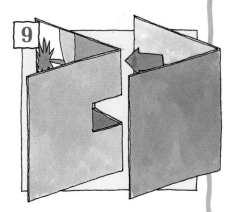

Glue the other piece of cardboard to the back —but don't put any glue on the center strip!

ZIGZAG CARDS

Fold, cut, and unfold—and a whole herd of elephants appears! Try cutting out a different design and you have a row of teddy bears, or a little train . . . .

The tomato card has a special surprise tucked into its front pocket—a pack of seeds that grow into beautiful plants!

1

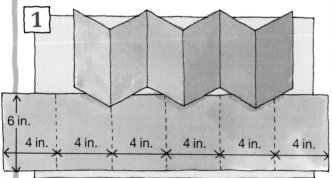

Take a strip of thin cardboard, measuring 24 by 6 inches. Divide it into six 4-inch sections with a ruler and pencil. Score along the lines, then fold the card into a zigzag.

2

Draw your design onto the front of the folded strip. Make sure the design touches both sides of the card for at least $\frac{1}{2}$ inch at each point, or it will all fall apart when you cut it out!

3

Cut out the design, then carefully unfold it again. Paint one side of the card, or glue down shapes cut from colored paper. Write your message on the back of the card.

Say It With Seeds!

Buy a pack of seeds. Cut and fold a zigzag (make it a little bigger than the pack). Cut a cardboard pocket for the seeds and glue it to the front.

On the inside, show what happens when you plant the seeds!

TOMATO

MOBILES

Yet another brilliant idea that's a lot easier than it looks. This type of card is very eye-catching because the mobile shape keeps swinging around in even the gentlest breeze.

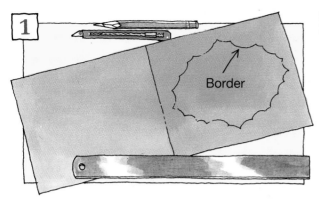

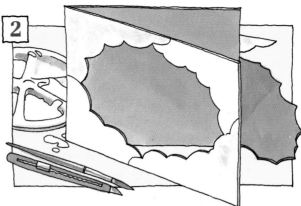

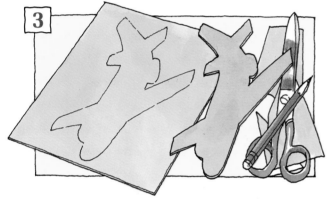

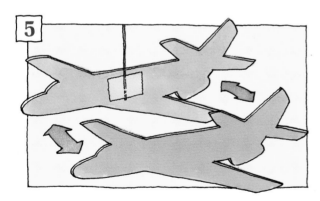

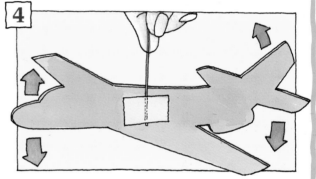

1 Cut out a rectangle of cardboard, and score a line down the middle. Draw a border on the front—the cards in the photo should give you some ideas.

2 Cut out the part inside the border and fold the card in half. Paint the front and insides of the card, or decorate them with paper shapes.

3 Cut out a shape from another piece of cardboard. Make sure that it fits within the border. Draw around it to make a second shape and cut this out, too.

4 Cut a piece of thread about 3 inches long. Tape it lightly to one of the shapes—alter the position until the shape balances from the thread.

5 Glue the second shape over the first so that the thread is trapped between them. Decorate both sides of the shape with paints or paper collage.

6 Tape the top of the thread inside the front of the card. Check that the shape can swing around without touching the border.

MOVING PICTURES

Pull the tab and watch the balloon glide across the sky!
For this design, you'll need one piece of cardboard measuring
8 x 6 inches and another measuring $16\frac{1}{2}$ x $6\frac{1}{2}$ inches. You'll also
need to cut out a narrow strip, 10 inches long and 1 inch wide.

1
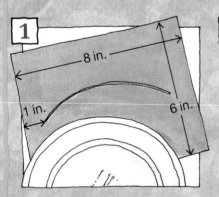

Cut a curved slot in the smaller piece of cardboard using a saucer as a guide. Leave 1 inch on both edges.

2

Decorate this piece, avoiding the curve. Draw and decorate the balloon on another piece, and cut it out.

3
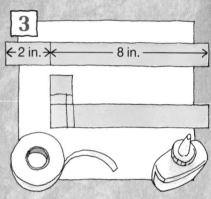

Cut the narrow strip into two pieces. Glue the pieces into an "L" shape, and tape over the corner.

4
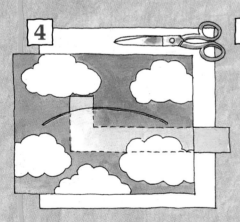

When the glue is dry, tuck the shorter length of the "L" through the slot from behind, as shown in the picture.

5

Glue the balloon to the top of the "L" shape. Check that it moves freely when you pull the other end of the strip.

6
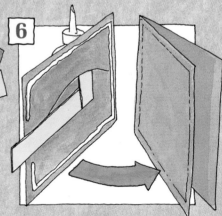

Fold the larger piece of cardboard, and glue the decorated piece to the front. Don't put glue near the "L" strip.

3

4

Cut the windowpanes from pieces of colored tissue paper or crepe paper. Put glue on one side of the cardboard and stick down the colored pieces— trim them so they don't overlap.

Fold a $15\frac{1}{3}$ x $7\frac{3}{4}$-inch piece of cardboard in half. Draw a $\frac{3}{4}$-inch border onto the front and cut out the middle. Glue your stained glass window to the back, as shown.

ZODIAC COLLAGE

Most of the cards in this book were decorated by gluing down pieces of colored paper. However, you could also use old magazines, newspapers, aluminum foil, postcards, stamps, scraps of fabric or wallpaper, dried beans or pasta, flowers or grasses, shells, nuts and bolts . . . the possibilities are endless!

Here's how to make a zodiac card from collage. There is a design for every star sign! Copy the shapes onto cardboard, or ask an adult to enlarge them on a photocopier.

Cut and fold a piece of cardboard—as big or as little as you like. Draw one of the zodiac signs onto the front. If you're using a photocopy, cut it out and glue it down.

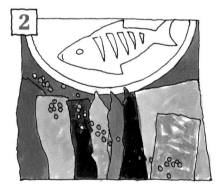

Sort out the materials you're going to use. Put glue on the design, a little at a time, and gradually cover it with your materials. Leave it to dry before sending.

Capricorn

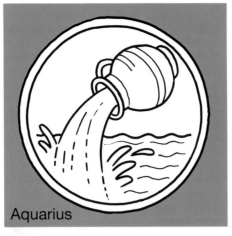

Aquarius

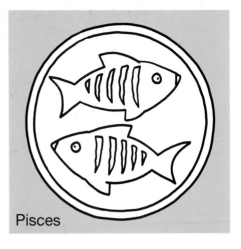

Pisces

Aries

Taurus

Gemini

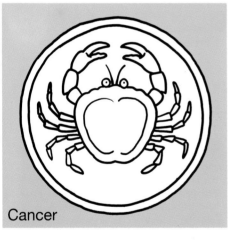

Cancer

Leo

Virgo

Libra

Scorpio

Sagittarius

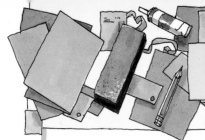

CHRISTMAS CARDS

At Christmastime, when you need to make a big batch of cards, the best idea is to set up a printing press and go into mass-production!

For a few special people, try making the cat-in-a-stocking to hang on the tree—or turn the page to discover how to make a jolly Santa who jumps right out of the envelope!

Printed Cards

Follow the instructions for printing cards on pages 92–93. Print simple shapes such as a tree, a present, or a star.

While your printing press is up and running, why not make your own wrapping paper—use wallpaper or brown wrapping paper.

Use scraps of cardboard for gift tags. Make holes with a hole punch, and thread with ribbon.

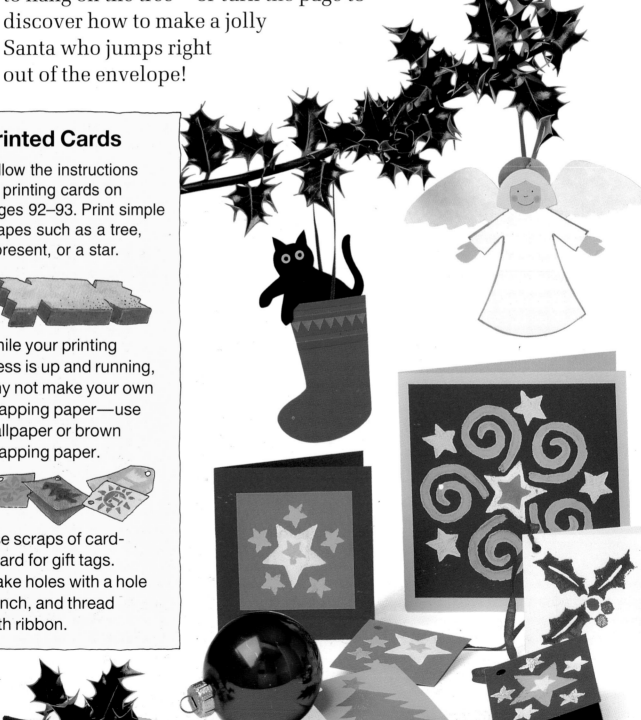

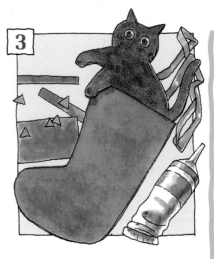

Christmas Cat

Fold a piece of thin, colored cardboard in half. Draw the stocking shape, with the folded edge as one side. Cut it out.

Glue the edges of the stocking together, but leave the top open. Draw and cut out a cat from black cardboard. Glue it in the stocking.

Decorate the card with bits of colored paper. Tape a loop of ribbon to the back, and write your Christmas greeting underneath.

All kinds of simple Christmas shapes can be used for your prints and tree decorations. How about stars, holly, snowpeople, or angels?

117

Pop-up Santa

Copy the diagram (shown right) onto a piece of red cardboard, using a pencil and ruler. Paint or decorate Santa's head and the chimney section.

Score and fold the cardboard in along the dotted lines, and tuck the Santa through the middle slit. The folded card should form a shape like the one shown in step 3.

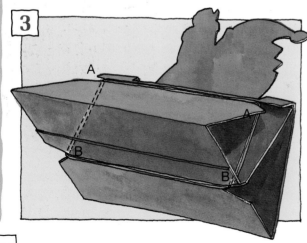

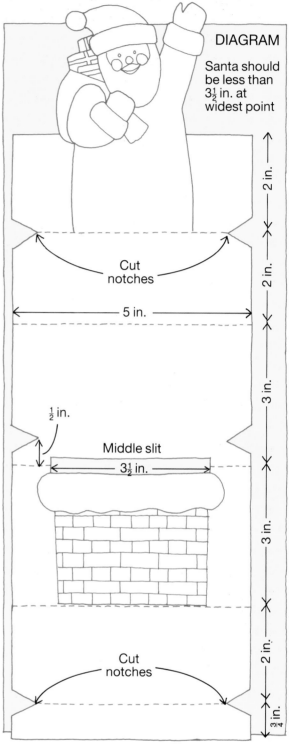

DIAGRAM

Santa should be less than $3\frac{1}{2}$ in. at widest point

2 in.

2 in.

5 in.

3 in.

$\frac{1}{2}$ in.

Middle slit

$3\frac{1}{2}$ in.

Cut notches

3 in.

Cut notches

2 in.

$\frac{3}{4}$ in.

Loop one end of a rubber band over the notches at the back (A), and loop the opposite end over the notches at the bottom (B). This may look tricky, but it's very simple once you get the hang of it!

The winged horse flies across the sky in the same way as the balloon. You could also try drawing a bird, a plane . . . or even your favorite superhero!

CARDS WITH FEET!

These cute 3-D cards can be folded flat for sending. The methods shown here can be adapted to make animals of all shapes and sizes—how about a tall giraffe, a plump hippo, or even a whole team of reindeer for Christmas?

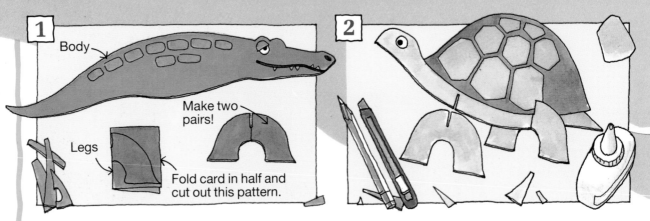

Crocodile and Turtle

Draw the turtle or crocodile's body onto stiff cardboard, and cut it out. Make two pairs of legs as shown.

Cut two $\frac{1}{2}$-inch slots in the body, and one into the top of each pair of legs. Decorate, and slot in the legs.

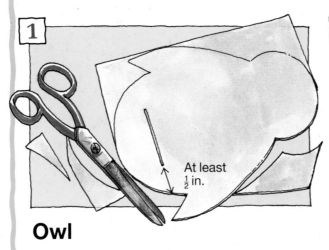

Owl

Draw the body onto cardboard and cut it out. Cut a slot across the bottom half, leaving at least $\frac{1}{2}$ inch between the slot and each edge.

Cut out and fold a shape like the one above for the feet and tail. Slot this through the body. Decorate the owl using paints or paper collage.

Decorate one side of your animal
card using paints or paper shapes.
Then write your message on the
other side—use a fountain pen, a
colored felt-tip, or, best of all, a
gold or silver pen.

111

WINDOW CARDS

"tained glass" cards look beautiful and
ysterious—they're often made at
ristmastime, but there's nothing
stop you from sending them in spring,
mmer, or fall!

"Bridges"

$\frac{3}{4}$ in.

Cut out a $6\frac{3}{4}$-inch square of cardboard. Draw a design onto the front,
leaving at least $\frac{3}{4}$ inch between it and
the edge. Leave "bridges" of at least
inch between the holes.

Cut out the holes for the "windowpanes" with a craft knife. If you cut
through a bridge by mistake,
fix it with tape.

4 To put the card into the envelope, gently squeeze the sides until it is flat.

When someone opens the envelope, the rubber band makes the Santa pop back up!

119

VALENTINE'S DAY

Here's a stylish valentine to make for the one you love (don't forget to add your secret message on the back)!
Start by cutting out a rectangle of colored cardboard measuring 7 x 4¾ inches. Then cut out a square of cardboard in another color measuring 4¾ x 4¾ inches.

Try dangling a tiny heart on a piece of thread inside the main shape.

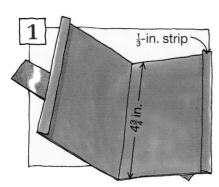

1

$\frac{1}{3}$-in. strip

$4\frac{3}{4}$ in.

Score and fold the larger piece of card-board down the middle. Then score a $\frac{1}{3}$-inch strip at each side and fold the strips toward you.

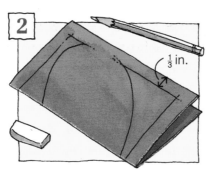

2

$\frac{1}{3}$ in.

Fold the smaller piece in half. Draw a border $\frac{1}{3}$ inch from the edges. Draw half of a heart shape, making the sides touch the border.

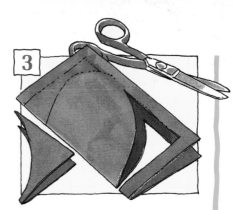

3

Cut out the area around the heart or, for a slightly different card, just cut out the heart. Both types are shown in the photo.

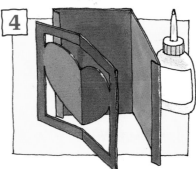

4

Glue the sides of the card to the folded strips on the larger card. Leave to dry before folding again.

To make a pair of tiny hearts, just cut out a single heart from the middle of the folded smaller card.

EASTER CHICKS

When you open the top half of this Easter egg, a bright yellow chick hatches out!

You'll need cardboard measuring $4\frac{1}{3}$ x 3 inches for each egg, and a 4-inch square of yellow cardboard for the chick. You'll also need a paper fastener to hold the egg together.

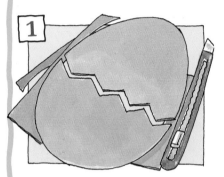

Cut out an egg shape from colored cardboard. Cut a zigzag across the middle.

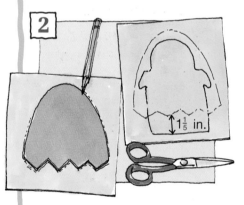

Place the top of the egg on the yellow square, and draw around it. Draw the chick inside the line, adding an extra $1\frac{1}{5}$ inch onto the bottom. Cut out the chick.

If fluffy chicks don't appeal, how about a baby dinosaur?

3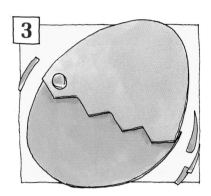

Overlap the two egg halves, and join them at one side with a paper fastener. Close the egg, and trim the edges to make a neat shape.

4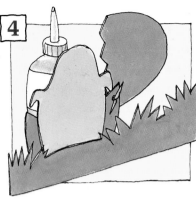

Glue the chick to the back of the bottom half of the egg. Cut out a strip of "grass," and glue this behind the bottom of the egg.

5

Cut and fold a $12\frac{1}{2}$ x $5\frac{1}{2}$- inch piece of cardboard. Glue the grass strip, the chick, and the bottom half of the egg to the front of the card.

Instead of step 5, you could make your egg stand up by itself—just glue a folded piece of cardboard to the back.

123

MORE IDEAS

You don't have to wait for a special occasion to send a card—it's a good way to keep in touch all year round!

Writing thank you letters doesn't have to be boring! Cut out a little card in the shape of the gift—then just scribble your note of thanks on the back.

Moving? Make some cards to let your friends know where your new home is!

Paper fastener

Pack some blank postcards and your paints or felt-tip pens next time you go on vacation—homemade postcards are a lot nicer than ones you can buy from souvenir shops!

STEP-BY-STEP

MAKING BOOKS

MAKING BOOKS

WHAT YOU NEED

First of all, you'll need to get together a basic bookmaker's kit like the one shown in the photo. You'll also need a thick piece of cardboard or masonite to protect your work surface from paint, cuts, and scratches.

Paper and Cardboard

You'll need plenty of thick paper or thin cardboard to make pages, and heavier board for hard covers.

Practice making books from scrap paper first. Then visit an art store to see the huge choice of paper and board available!

Glue

White glue or paste is good for sticking paper and cardboard together, and for making collages.

For more heavy-duty gluing (attaching a cover, for example), use safe household glues— *not* superglue.

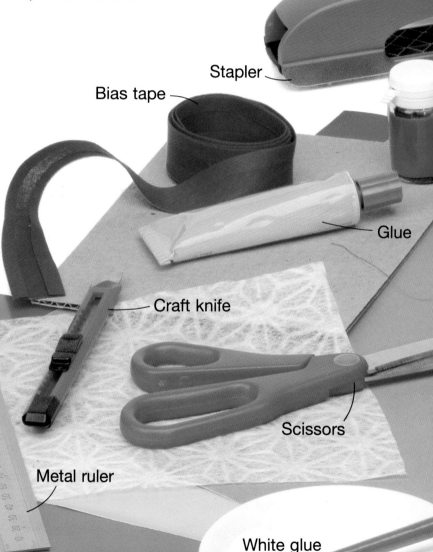

Stapler

Bias tape

Glue

Craft knife

Scissors

Metal ruler

White glue

Ribbon

Tools of the Trade

To sew the pages of your books, you'll need a big darning needle, some strong thread, and a pair of scissors. A stapler can also be used to make some simple books.

You'll need a craft knife and a metal ruler to cut the cardboard and paper. *Always* make sure an adult is around to watch and help when you're doing any cutting.

Other Things

Among the other things you'll need are: poster paints, felt-tip pens, and colored pencils for coloring your books; strips of strong tape or bias binding for making hard covers; scraps of ribbon; colored fabric and paper; and a few large spring clips.

Poster paints

Strong thread

Spring clip

Paper and cardboard

Pencils

Felt-tip pens

Cotton binding

Brushes

String

129

MAKING BOOKS

The following pages show you how to make books of all shapes and sizes—just follow the step-by-step instructions carefully. Here are some tips on cutting and folding, along with some of the terms you'll meet throughout the book.

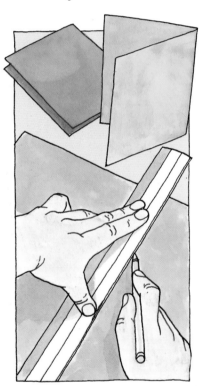

The *illustrations* are the pictures in your book.

A *spread* is two pages that face each other.

The *text* is all the words in the book.

The *heading* is usually bigger than the other words on the page.

Folding

Folding cardboard and thick paper is easier if you run a used-up ballpoint (or the back of your craft knife) lightly over the line first—this is called *scoring*.

Endpapers are stuck between the covers and the first and last pages of the book.

Spine

Front
cover

The *gutter* runs down
the middle of the spread.

Although the books
shown on the following
pages come in many
different shapes and
sizes, the basic parts are
the same. These parts
are labeled here.

Cutting

Craft knives are very
sharp and need to be
handled with care!
Don't press too
hard—several light
strokes are best. A metal
ruler will help you to keep
the lines straight.

FOLDERS AND WALLETS

Folders and wallets have lots of different uses—unlike real books, you can change the contents as often as you like! You can also tuck in extra bits and pieces, such as maps, photos, magazine clippings—even a booklet or two.

Folder

Fold a big piece of fairly stiff cardboard in half (see the notes on folding and scoring on page 130).

Cut another piece slightly smaller than one half of the folder, and with flaps on two sides.

Cut several more pieces of cardboard, each smaller than the last. Fold the flaps and glue them inside the folder as shown. Leave to dry.

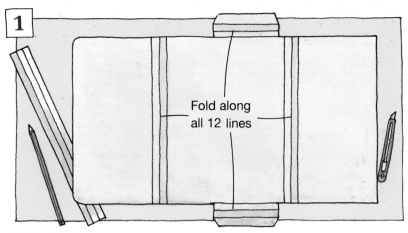

Wallet

With a pencil and a ruler, copy the pattern shown above onto a sheet of thick paper or thin cardboard.

Cut it out, using a ruler and a craft knife. Score all the inside lines with an old ballpoint, or the back of the craft knife.

Fold along the lines. Make the middle fold first, then fold in the opposite direction along the two other folds.

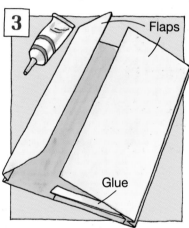

To finish your wallet, glue the top of the side flaps inside the bottom fold, as shown.

Left: A colorful selection of wallets and folders made from cardboard.

133

SEWING THE PAGES

The following pages show three different ways of sewing the pages of your book.

If you want to add a cover (see pages 138–139) to the books shown in methods A and B, you must strengthen the spine with a strip of cardboard. However, if you don't want a hard cover, you can leave this out.

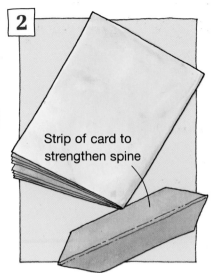

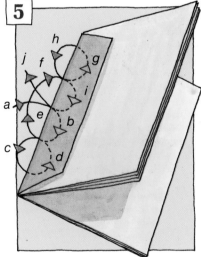

Method A

Take up to six pieces of heavy paper or thin cardboard. Fold them in the middle, and stack them inside each other to make a book.

Cut a strip of cardboard the same length as your book. Trim the top and bottom diagonally, as shown, and fold around the spine of your book.

Hold the pages of your book tightly in place with a spring clip. Then mark the middle point along the gutter with a ruler and pencil.

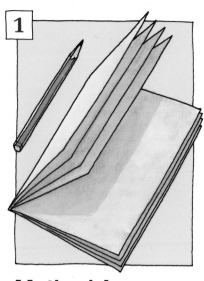

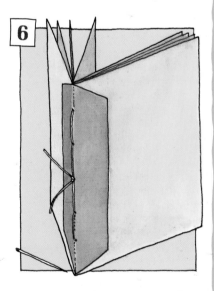

Add two more marks on each side of the middle mark, making them the same distance apart. Make a hole through the pencil marks with a darning needle.

Push the needle and thread through the middle mark, starting from the outside. Keep sewing in and out, following the direction shown above.

You should end up with two loose ends of thread outside the spine, as here. Tie them together with a double knot in the middle, and trim the ends with scissors.

Method B

Fold a big piece of paper in half several times (two folds make an 8-page book, three folds make a 16-page book, and four folds make 32 pages). Add a strip of cardboard along the spine as shown in step 2 of method A (see page 135).

Sew exactly as shown for method A. With a ruler and craft knife, neatly trim all the edges except the spine.

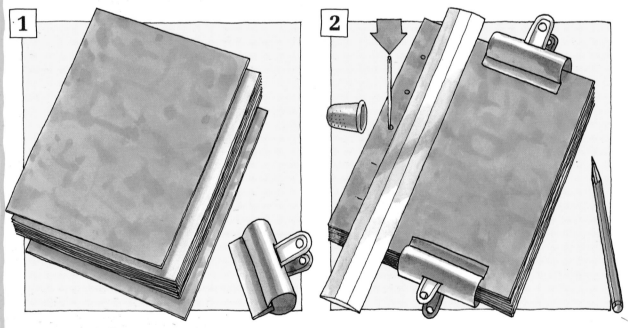

Method C

Take several sheets of paper of the same size, and stack them in a pile. Cut two cardboard covers and place them at the top and bottom of the pile. Hold everything in place with spring clips.

With a ruler and pencil, draw a line $1/4$ inch in from the spine. Mark five points along the line, all the same distance apart, and pierce them with a darning needle.

3

Thread the needle with strong thread. Sew around the spine in the direction shown in the picture.

4

Then sew back along the spine in the opposite direction. Tie the two loose ends together.

MAKING COVERS

The simplest kind of cover to make is a soft cardboard wrapper. However, if you want the book to be really strong and long-lasting, you could try gluing the pages into a hard cover, with a spine made from cotton binding or bias tape.

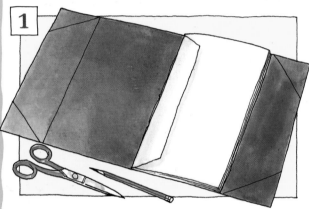

Wrapper Cover

Measure and cut out a piece of thick paper the same height as the pages of your book, but twice as wide, and with a wide flap at each end.

Trim the wrapper flaps top and bottom, then score and fold them in. Fold the wrapper in half, and lay the book inside.

Cut a flap in the middle of the front and back pages. Fold and tuck in the cover flaps, as shown.

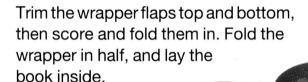

1

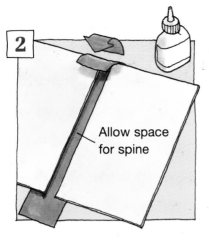

2

Allow space for spine

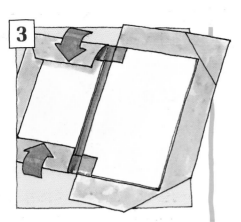

3

Hard Cover

Cut out two pieces of strong cardboard. Make them about $^{3}/_{16}$ inch wider than the pages of your book on all sides.

Glue the pieces onto a strip of cloth, allowing an extra $1^{1}/_{2}$ inches at the top and bottom. Fold the extra pieces over and glue.

Cut two pieces of paper, 2 inches wider than the boards on the top, outer, and bottom edges. Trim the corners of the papers and glue to the boards as shown.

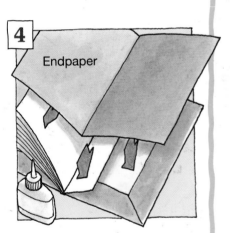

4

Endpaper

Glue the back of the piece of strengthening board to the cover. Then glue the first and last pages of the book to the inside of the covers. Or, cut two separate endpapers from colored paper and glue them between the cover and the book.

PRINTING PATTERNS

Try printing designs onto your covers—use poster paints for the stencils and printing blocks, and oil paints for marbling.

You can also make beautiful patterned endpapers in the same way, or even print directly onto the pages of your book.

Stenciling

Draw a design on stenciling board or ordinary thin cardboard. Carefully cut out the holes with a craft knife.

Hold the board down on the cover and dab thick poster paint over the holes with a piece of sponge or a stenciling brush.

Printing Blocks

Cut some shapes out of foam rubber and glue them to thick squares of wood or cardboard.

Dip the shapes into thick paint and press them down to print. When the paint is dry, you could add some extra details by using a darker color.

Marbling

Half-fill a wide tray with water. Mix some oil paint with mineral spirits until runny, then dribble them across the water.

Swirl the water gently with a clean brush, then lay a sheet of paper on top.

Smooth carefully, lift off, and leave to dry.

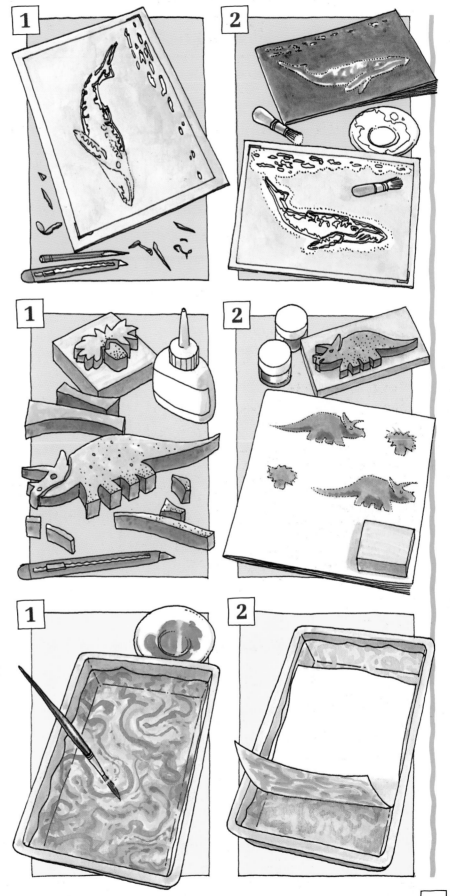

141

COLLAGE COVERS

Magazines, newspapers, and greeting cards can all be cut up and glued to your covers to make a collage. You can also use bits of junk to make pictures and patterns—they look best if you paint them afterward. A coat of clear varnish will stop the paint from rubbing off the covers.

Collage Castle

This castle was made from tree bark, aluminum foil, sandpaper, toothpicks, pencils, and bamboo— but you could use all kinds of spare junk! The moon was made from half a cashew nut.

Once the glue was dry, the castle was painted silver-gray.

Découpage

Cut pictures out of old wrapping paper, magazines, or news-papers, and glue them to your cover to make an overlapping pattern.

Look for interesting colors, pictures, and shades. Try tearing some of the pages—this gives a softer edge than cutting them.

Antique Book

Cut out some shapes from cardboard and some short lengths of string. Glue them to the cover in a pattern.

Brush black paint along the raised edges, then leave to dry. Rub gold paint over the cover with a dry brush.

BOOKMARKS

Make bookmarks from leftover cardboard! If your book has a theme, your bookmark could match it— for example, a monster bookmark could hang over the pages of a scary story!

1 Draw and cut a bookmark out of cardboard. Paint it, or decorate it by gluing on some cardboard shapes. Draw a flap and cut it out with a craft knife.

2 Slot the flap over a page in your book. You could also make a flap by gluing on an extra piece of cardboard (like the parrot's wing, see right)—only the top should be glued to the bookmark.

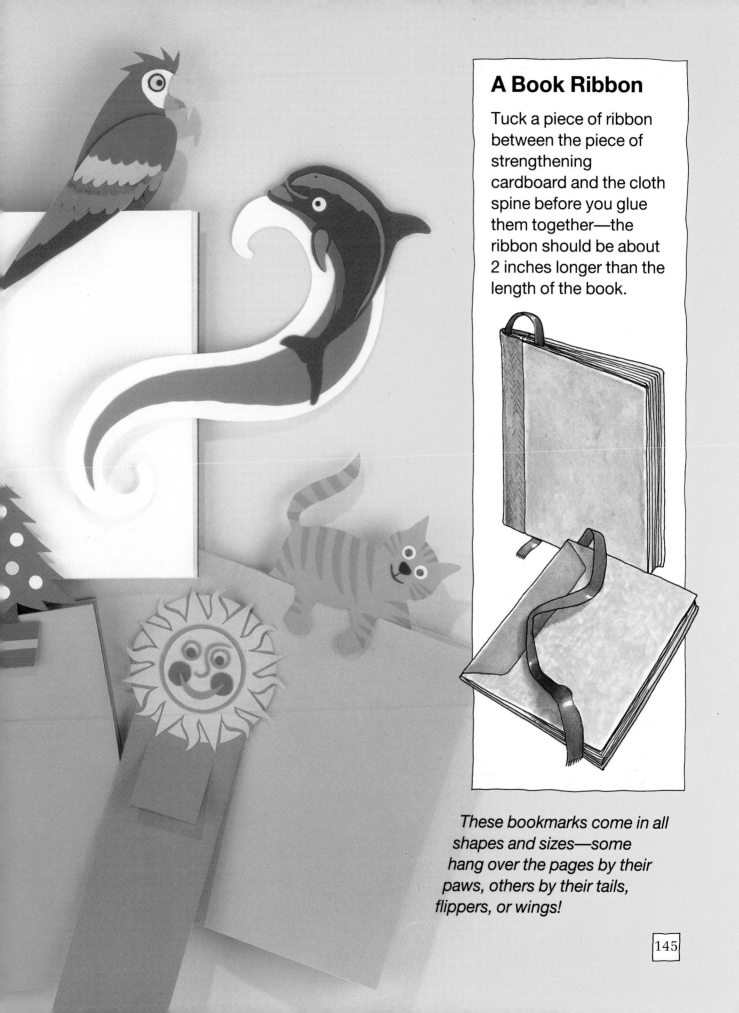

A Book Ribbon

Tuck a piece of ribbon between the piece of strengthening cardboard and the cloth spine before you glue them together—the ribbon should be about 2 inches longer than the length of the book.

These bookmarks come in all shapes and sizes—some hang over the pages by their paws, others by their tails, flippers, or wings!

DESIGNING BOOKS

Now that you've made your book, what are you going to do with it? You may want to use the book as a diary or a notebook, or to give it to someone as a gift. On the other hand, you could use it to write and illustrate a story, a poem, or anything else at all. Here's how you go about it.

Count how many pages you have in your book, then draw them on a piece of paper. This is called a *page plan*. It will help you to work out where you want your text and illustrations to go.

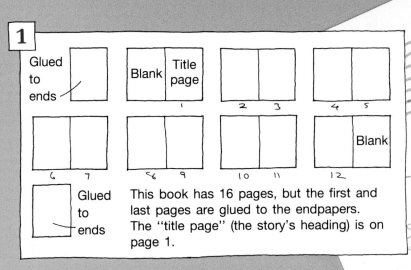

1

Glued to ends

Blank | Title page — 1

2 | 3

4 | 5

6 | 7

Glued to ends

8 | 9

10 | 11

12 | Blank

This book has 16 pages, but the first and last pages are glued to the endpapers. The "title page" (the story's heading) is on page 1.

2

Decide how many lines of text to put on each page. Some pages can have more text than others, as you can see from the designs shown here.

3

Plan where your text and illustrations will go.

4

Draw a writing guide on cardboard (the same size as a page from your book). Use a black pen, and keep the spaces between the lines equal.

Vary the position of the text and pictures—some ideas are shown here.

5

Write the words and pictures lightly in your book in pencil. Slip the writing guide under the page to help keep the lines of text even.

ADDING PICTURES

When you're happy with the way your designs look, you can use your pens and paints to fill in the words and pictures.

Do the illustrations first, using some of the suggestions on these pages. Then carefully write the words around the pictures.

The dinosaur spreads below were painted, while the planets and rockets were made by gluing on pieces of cardboard and paper.

The spread on the far right shows how magazines can be cut up and arranged to make collage pictures.

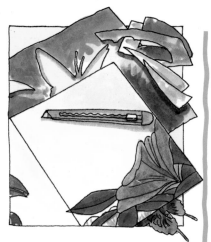

Painting

You can draw or paint the illustrations directly onto the pages. Or trace some pictures from your favorite books and magazines and color them in.

Paper Shapes

Cut shapes from cardboard or paper and glue them to the pages to make pictures (most of the photos in this book show books illustrated in this way).

Collage

Cut pictures from old color magazines and glue them into your book.

You could also use newspapers, photos you've taken yourself, or photocopies.

NOVELTY NOTEBOOKS

Notebooks can be quickly sewn or stapled to make presents for birthdays or Christmas—they can be any shape or size, as long as you remember to leave most of the folded edge uncut. You can either leave the insides blank, or write in special messages or information.

1 Fold several sheets of thick paper together. Draw on the design for your book, and sew down the middle of the pages (see page 135).

2 Cut around the outline of the notebook as shown. Make sure you don't cut any of the thread that holds the spine of the book together.

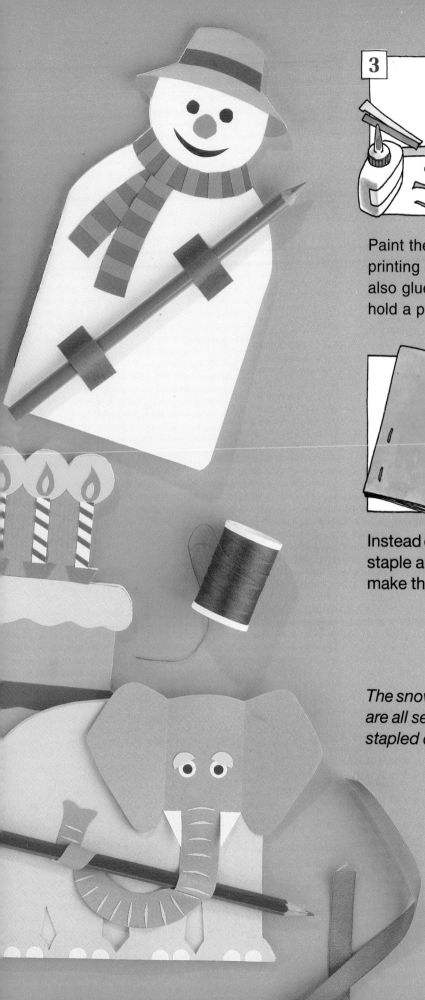

3

Paint the front, or use some of the printing ideas on page 141. You could also glue on loops of cardboard to hold a pen or pencil.

Instead of sewing the books, you could staple along the spine—as we did to make the birthday cake book.

The snowman, elephant, and sunflower are all sewn. The birthday cake book is stapled down the side.

To make the butterfly, cut several wing-shaped pages and sew down the middle. Cut out the body separately, and glue it over the stitches.

ZIGZAG BOOKS

Zigzag books don't need any sewing! They can be written and read just like ordinary books, or unfolded and pinned to the wall to make a frieze.

These books look best if you make them out of heavy paper or thin cardboard.

1

2

Simple Zigzag

Divide a long strip of thin cardboard or thick paper into equal parts using a ruler and a pencil.

Fold the paper into a zigzag. Then add your illustrations and text (if any).

Decorate both sides— use them to make long, foldout friezes or to tell a story.

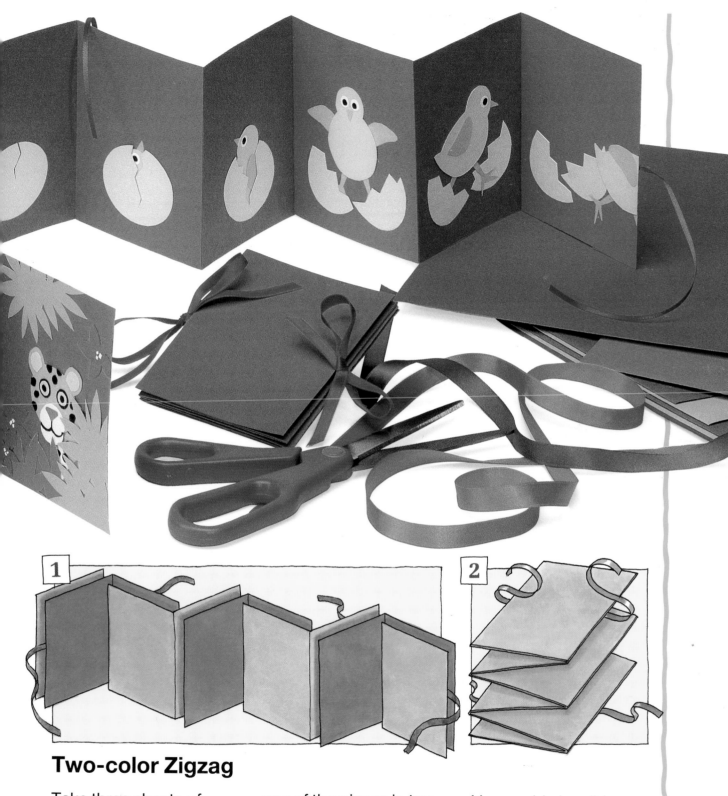

Two-color Zigzag

Take three sheets of paper in one color and three in another color. Fold them in half, and cut one of the pieces in two. Glue together to make a zigzag, with the two cut pieces at each end.

You could glue ribbon under the end pieces to tie up the zigzag, as shown.

POP-UP BOOKS

How about having pop-up pictures in your books? They look very impressive, but aren't that difficult to make. Like the flaps and moving parts on pages 157–160, pop-ups work best in books with fewer than ten pages made of thin cardboard.

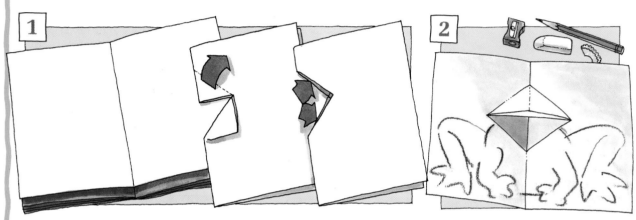

1

2

Mouths and Beaks

Cut a piece of cardboard the same size as a spread in your book. Fold the

paper, and cut a slit near the middle. Fold back the flaps, and tuck in.

When you open the page, the flaps will open like a mouth or beak!

3

Color the picture, then glue the page into your book. Don't put any glue on the back of the mouth or beak.

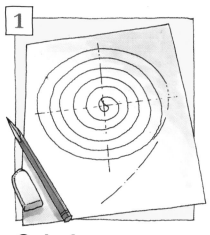

1

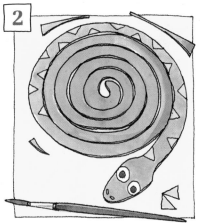

2

3

Spirals

Draw a circle on some thin cardboard, slightly smaller than a page from your book. Draw a spiral inside the circle.

Draw a snake's head at the outer edge of the circle, as shown. Cut around all the lines with scissors.

Use paints, felt-tip pens, or bits of colored paper to decorate the snake and to make a colorful jungle background.

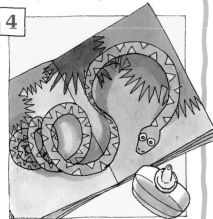

4

Glue the *back* of the snake's head to the right-hand page. Put a dab of glue on the *top* of its tail. Shut the book, press together, then open and leave to dry.

You can glue on extra details made from cardboard, such as this frog's bulging eyes!

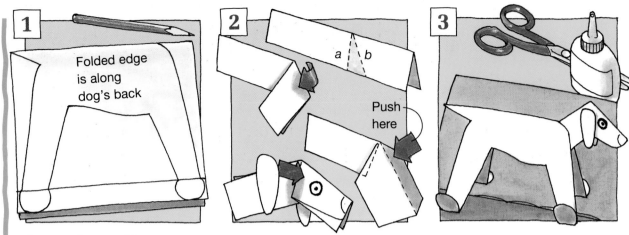

Stand-up Dog

Fold a 3 x 5½-inch piece of cardboard in half. Draw the shape of the dog's body and cut it out so that the folded edge is along the dog's back.

Fold a 1½ x 3½-inch piece of cardboard in half. Make folds *a* and *b*. Open and push down to make the head. Cut and glue on the ears.

Glue the neck into the body. Fold the paws back on one side, and glue the undersides to one of the pages, ½ inch from the gutter.

Fold back the paws on the other side. Dab the undersides with glue, and fold the facing page on top of them.

You can decorate your stand-up animals before gluing them into your book. This dog's spots were made with a hole-puncher and then glued to the body.

FLAPS AND MOVERS

You can add even more fun and excitement to your books by making flaps that open, holes to peek through, and wheels that turn! You could also use these methods to make really special greeting cards.

Flaps

Simple doors and windows can be glued straight into your book.

You can also cut flaps from a separate page of cardboard, and glue the page into the book.

Peepholes

Peepholes such as keyholes and window panes can be cut from the cover or inside pages to show part of the picture on the page underneath.

Mix and Match

Cut a small book into three sections. Draw a figure on the front. Open the flaps, and mark where the neck and legs join. Draw a new figure on each page.

157

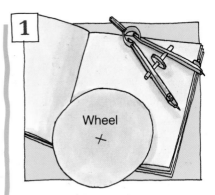

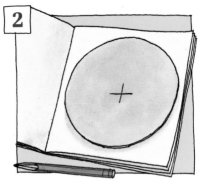

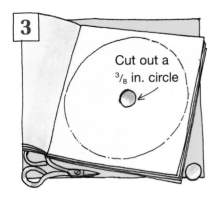

Wheels

Cut out a cardboard wheel ³/₈-inch smaller than a page in your book.

Put the wheel on the page, and draw around it. Mark both centers.

Measure a ³/₈-inch circle around the mark on the page and cut it out.

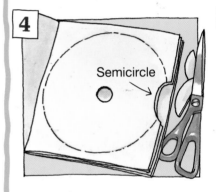

Cut a semicircle from the page edge, and also from the page beneath it.

Cut out a window, leaving ³/₈ inch between the outer edge of the

circle and the window, and ³/₈-inch between the window and the center.

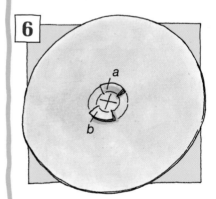

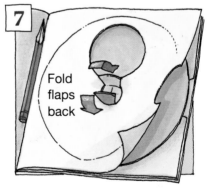

Draw a ³/₄-inch circle in the middle of the wheel, with a ³/₈-inch circle inside it. Cut and fold up flaps *a* and *b* as shown.

Lay the wheel under the page, and push the flaps through the hole. Turn the wheel around, and draw inside the window.

Glue the edges of the page to the one underneath. Then glue another small circle to the flaps— *not* to the page.

Your wheel could show ghosts in a haunted castle . . . or a changing view from a porthole!

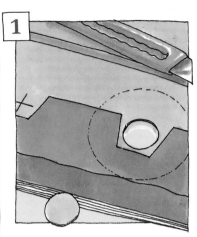

1

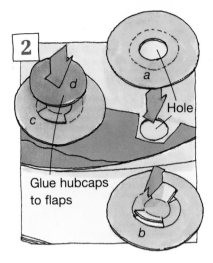

2

Hole

Glue hubcaps
to flaps

a
b
c
d

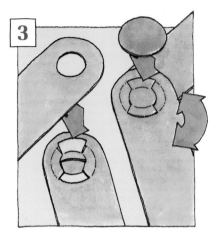

3

Moving Machines

Draw a machine onto a
page in your book, or
make the picture from
shapes cut from
cardboard. Draw the
outline of a wheel, and
cut a ³⁄₈-inch circle from
the middle of the wheel.

Cut two cardboard
wheels, one with flaps
(see page 158), and one
with a ³⁄₈-inch hole in the
center. Assemble as
shown. Cut a hubcap from
cardboard, and glue it
onto the flaps.

You can join other
moving parts in the same
way. Just cut a hole in
one of the parts, and
flaps in the other. Slot
together as shown, and
cover with circles cut
from cardboard.

PEEK-IN BOOKS

Here's a very special bookmaking project, and once again, it's much simpler than it looks! The book has five spreads, so if you want to use it for a story or a poem, you'll have to divide your text into five separate sections.

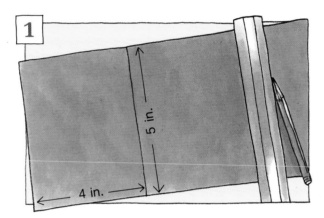

To make the background for the book, cut a strip of thin cardboard 5 x 40 inches. Use a ruler to divide it into ten pages, each 4 inches wide.

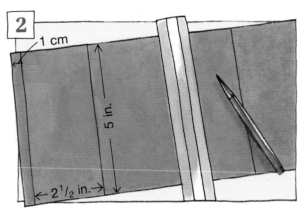

Cut a strip measuring 5 x 25 inches for the foreground. Allow a $\frac{1}{2}$-inch flap at each end. Divide the rest of the strip into ten pages, each $2\frac{1}{2}$ inches wide.

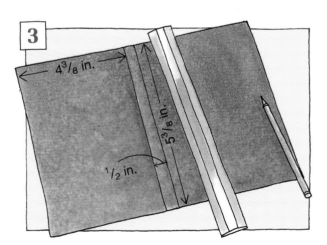

Cut a slightly thicker piece of cardboard for the cover ($5\frac{3}{8}$ x $9\frac{1}{4}$ inches). Measure a spine $\frac{1}{2}$ inch wide down the middle and score along the lines.

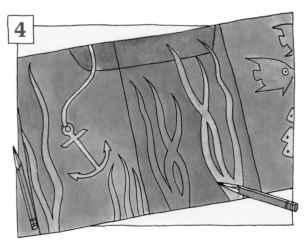

Draw and color the five background spreads (each spread is made up of two pages). It's best to keep these pictures quite simple.

You can use paint to decorate the foreground and background, or glue shapes cut from cardboard, as shown here.

5

Plan illustrations for the five foreground spreads, allowing for peepholes in each one. Paint the spreads, or glue on cutout pictures.

6

Fold both the strips carefully into zig-zags, as shown above. Fold the two $\frac{1}{2}$-inch flaps at both ends of the foreground strip outward.

7 Put short lengths of ribbon between the cover and the first and last pages of the background strip, then glue the pages to the cover.

8 Put a thin line of glue down all the folded edges of the background strip and on the flaps of the foreground. Glue the two strips together.

163

MORE IDEAS

Several books can be put into a box called a *slipcase*. Cut the case shape shown from cardboard, using the size of the books as a guide.

    The length and width of the case should be about $\frac{1}{2}$ inch longer than the books, and the depth should be $\frac{1}{2}$ inch wider than the spines of the books when they're stacked together. Add flaps, fold up, and glue into a case.

Width

Length

Depth

Flaps

Slipcase

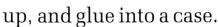

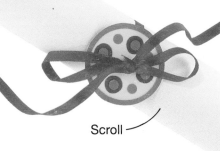

Scroll

Scrolls were among the earliest types of book. Make one by rolling up a sheet of paper and tying with ribbon—add a "seal" cut from cardboard, if you like.

Try gluing a magnet to the back of a tiny book, and sticking it on the fridge!

Fridge magnet notebook